Collaborating through Virtual Communities
Using Cloud Technology

COLLABORATING THROUGH
VIRTUAL COMMUNITIES
USING CLOUD TECHNOLOGY

DIANE STOTTLEMYER

Westphalia Press
An Imprint of the Policy Studies Organization
Washington, DC
2016

Westphalia Press
An imprint of Policy Studies Organization
1527 New Hampshire Ave., NW
Washington, D.C. 20036
info@ipsonet.org

ISBN-10: 1-63391-409-7
ISBN-13: 978-1-63391-409-4

Cover and interior design by Jeffrey Barnes
jbarnesbook.design

Daniel Gutierrez-Sandoval, Executive Director
PSO and Westphalia Press

Updated material and comments on this edition
can be found at the Westphalia Press website:
www.westphaliapress.org

INTRODUCTION

Colleges and universities need to keep up with the latest techniques in communication so that when students begin their educational pursuits they are using the up-to-date technology. Not all colleges and universities have the flexibility and budgets to keep current on all forms of technologies but being able to provide students with available options will help colleges and universities to increase student population. Colleges and universities have different options and not all technologies are costly to implement. The key question is: Once students are admitted and enrolled, can the colleges and universities keep them engaged in their academic pursuits? This can be a challenge; however, by offering new technological advances, this makes the offer and acceptance more binding since students want to be socially connected.

The virtual community can be a pretty powerful tool for communicating in today's socially networked environment. There are many faces of socially connected networks that include Facebook, Myspace, or LinkedIn. Providing students an area where academic issues and discussions can ensue can encourage academic development. Developing a virtual community using a cloud service can socially increase networking interaction. This networking approach can also increase the performance of students and provide the services that the school may be able to offer at a lower cost to students. This collaborative approach to learning can be useful for students, teachers, and staff as an interactive collaborative approach to virtual education.

This book includes discussions and evaluation of virtual communities, cloud technology, use of virtual communities, challenges, advantages, e-collaboration, development, quality assurance planning, and future trends. The goal is to provide an introduction of the different areas noted above and plant a seed for considering how various virtual approaches to education could benefit the classroom.

CHAPTER 1.
VIRTUAL COMMUNITIES USING CLOUD TECHNOLOGY

Developing alternative approaches to education has become more and more predominant and has opened the door to learning in new environments. The purpose of this monograph is to provide readers with information that teachers, students, and staff can use for developing virtual communities using cloud technology. Teachers, students, and staff can develop a community of learning while sharing information and data. This development can be based on best practices that are established for a virtual community. Cloud technology can be an asset for the storage of data and information that teachers, students, and staff can use since space may be limited on the schools servers. Information that has a focus on big data can become increasingly difficult to manage so data and the cloud may be considered a symbiotic pivotal technology for managing a large amount of data.

Educational institutions rely on a large amount of data and the cloud has become an alternative approach for storage as well as assisting virtual communities when setting up a large amount of archived data. As cloud technology progresses, this will change how educational institutions evaluate current and future technologies. This will also change how schools store and archive data and information that is needed for students and teachers. It is important that schools keep current with alternative approaches to new technology while maintaining a budget that fits into the guidelines of the schools structure. It is important to continually look for ways to improve technology, communication, and collaboration in the school's environment because teachers and students need to be able to understand current and future trends.

Cloud technology is not only the ability to improve on technology and the way data is stored, but it is also a way to look for ways to improve interaction using a collaborative approach to other student's teachers and outside like-interest groups. Collaborating through virtual communities using cloud technology is an area of interest that will continue to grow because of the increased use of social media. More and more colleges and universities are working toward moving their businesses and curriculum to virtual communities and a cost-effective method is needed to make sure that this can happen. Information can be developed using an e-collaborating effort through virtual communities using cloud technology as a possible solution for advancing communication.

Cloud computing is no longer a trend but a reality so that schools can develop an approach of communication and information storage that can become a reality. Because of the increase in storage, a solution of cloud technology for data warehousing is possible. In this monograph, methods of e-collaborating, development of virual communities, cloud technology, and how cloud technology can be used for educational institutions will be discussed. Also, there will be an explanation of how e-collaboration can help improve the communication of virtual communities through cloud technology. First, it is important to understand what a virtual community is and what are its uses.

WHAT IS A VIRTUAL COMMUNITY?

A virtual community is a group of individuals who want to meet to share ideas, information, and collaborate on various topics. The virtual community is based on what the participants of the community consider a common interest. There are many areas and topics that can be specific for a virtual community and can be beneficial not only to students but also to teachers and staff. Generally, virtual communities are set up as a meeting place where individuals can collaborate, meet, and share virtual ideas. Wesner and Hobgood (2012) noted that virtual collaboration is an important step in managing a team and working toward encouraging participation between individuals. If teachers feel that additional collaboration is needed, then they can encourage the development of a virtual team for their classes. The virtual team may work on specific areas and topics related to a common area that may include specific discussions, including sharing relative experience.

Collaboration between individuals in a virtual community can help the community grow and thrive. "This growing interest in the importance

2

of collaborative skills and competencies is only magnified by the recent growth in the number of geographically dispersed teams in today's organizations and, in particular, virtual teams" (Wesner & Hobgood, 2012, pp. 29–30). As virtual communities grow in size, international interest can increase the size of the community, and, by using cloud technology, the increased interest can be managed effectively and efficiently.

Since everyone does not use the same methods of communication, it is necessary to understand the different types of communication devices that can be used and adapted to the virtual environment as well as the cloud. Figure 1 provides a representation of different ways of creating a virtual community using the cloud. Everyone does not use a laptop or a computer. There may also be mobile devices, tablets, and desktops that individuals may use to interact in the virtual community using cloud technology.

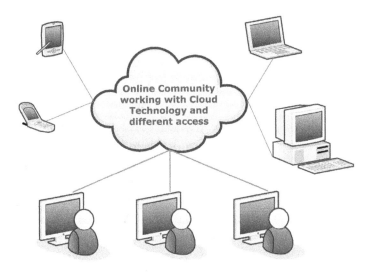

Figure 1. The Virtual Community Working in the Cloud

A collaborative approach is important for the virtual community, and new ways of communication are important to consider as technology continues to grow and advance. This collaborative approach is also needed as teachers determine the best approach to deliver the curriculum as an expansion to the virtual and traditional classroom. As teachers prepare their lesson plans, they need to build in the extension of the lesson to include how students can use the virtual classroom as a way to continue the interaction that is established in the classroom. This continuous interaction can be useful for both students and teachers as a means to expand on difficult or challenging topics. Teachers establish the goals and objectives so that the community can benefit with extended learning activities, increasing a collaborative effort. An interesting simulation was developed that Wesner and Hobgood (2012) discussed in the article "Virtual collaboration: Exploring the process and technology in a graduate course." They noted that a virtual environment can be evaluated and participants can survive in a virtual environment. As part of the evaluation, there was an analysis on how the students felt about the environment and whether it impacted their success as students. What was interesting to note is that not only the students developed and analyzed their experience but also the teachers evaluated their experience and compared their experience to those of the students. This can be beneficial particularly if changes need to be made for current and future courses. Continuous evaluation as well as continuous improvement can help move the technology forward while looking for new and improved ways to communicate.

Coming together as a group and collaborating about topics of interest are essential in an educational setting. Gupta and Kim (2004) discussed how virtual communities can be used to come together, share information, and discuss topics that are of interest to each other. In order for the virtual community to survive, there needs to be commitment and collaboration to help the community to grow while providing information for global environments. If a virtual community is developed and used as part of the collaboration process in a classroom, it would be benefical to have someone to manage and evaluate the discussion boards in the virtual community. Monitoring the virtual environment is needed so that there is progress and continual growth in the virtual environment. Plans for housing the information and data collected are necessary so that archives can be produced, shared, and stored for future access. A successful virtual community should have goals and objectives that include monitoring and archiving data that can be established by a teacher. A teacher can act as a focal point in order for the community to reach their goals and objectives for the virtual community.

A virtual community is beneficial because of the impact it has on a virtual classroom. Teachers want students to collaborate and share their experience. This sharing of knowledge from a classroom perspective may be more beneficial in an informal and open environment such as a virtual community. When there is an open and collaborative approach to learning, not only the virtual environment but also a learning environment with addtional resources for teachers and students is created. Understanding how a virtual community is set up and the type of software that is necessary for that purpose is important when evaluating the goals and objectives of the virtual community, for example, what are the best connections available for the virtual community, what are the best times to meet, who should be involved, is there a schedule, and what is the current agenda. These are all important areas. A virtual community plan should be developed in such a manner that the community does not waste time when their members meet and the meeting is productive (Gupta & Kim, 2004).

As cloud computing continues to grow, Divya and Prakasam noted, "Cloud computing is becoming an attractive technology due to its dynamic scalability and effective use of the resources; it can be utilized under circumstances where the availability of resources is limited" (Divya & Prakasam, 2015, p. 29). Not all educational institutions have unlimited budgets to operate extra curricular events such as a virtual cloud community. Therefore, looking for cost-effective tools and software is important. This is where cloud computing can be advantageous and benefit the teachers and the students. Since education is an area where resources are limited, the cloud environment has increased its appeal to use it as a platform. Divya and Prakasam (2015) suggested that there were six areas that should be the part of the cloud based e-learning area:

- Student management
- Staff management
- Course management
- File management
- Assessment management
- Virtual interaction

Student management is an important area and is necessary for those who are active in the community and are able to see that active participation occurs. If there is no active participation, it would be necessary to look for problems associated with participation. Another area of concern is whether there is enough staff to manage the community. Staff can also be used to determine how to increase participation that will provide benefits for a collaborative envirionment.

If the virtual community is expected to be useful, there should also be an evaluation of course and file management. In order to better assess the effectiveness of the information in the cloud enviroment, regular monitoring of class material and housing files for future virtual community activity is needed. Assessment management can be used to determine whether information is useful and if changes are necessary. A virtual community can benefit from the contiual evaluation and assessment of the effectivness of the materials and data. By using student, staff, course file assessment and management, and virtual interaction, this provides a basis for evaluating the effectiveness of the virtual community as well as determining if and when changes need to be made.

A process such as the PDCA (Plan, Do, Check, and Act) would be a useful tool to evaluate when changes need to be made. Note in Figure 2 how the PDCA cycle provides a sequential approach to evaluating a process or a problem. The PDCA is not only an important process for evaluating and assessing improvement but it can also be used to determine the need for continuous improvement.

The first phase of the PDCA cycle or "P" is the "Planning" phase. This phase may include a change, an update, or a complete evaluation of a new project. The "D" in the PDCA cycle is the "Do" phase, and this phase is used to evaluate the process and to work through the planning and testing of changes. The "C" or "Check" is used to analyze, test, and evaluate what has been developed in the "Do" phase as well as determining whether the plan is working fine. Finally, the "A," the "Act" phase, is required to evaluate whether the process changes work, is it necessary to go through the process again, or is the process changes ready to be put into place (American Society for Quality, 2016).

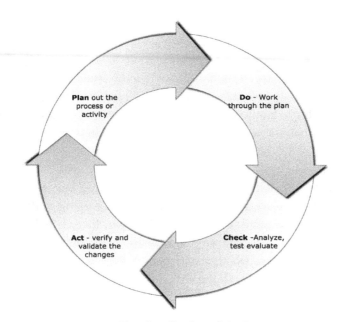

Figure 2. Plan, Do, Check, and Act Process

When applying the PDCA process, it is important to determine the effectiveness of the virtual community for teachers, students, and staff, and apply the following steps in the cycle:

(1) Plan how to develop the community. Determine who should be involved, how large the community should be, budget for the community, cloud technology, and the starting date of the project. The use of a Gantt chart as a project planning schedule tool would be useful to plan out the activities. This tool can also be used to determine timelines and responsibility for those involved.

(2) In the "Do" phase, the development of the community will begin, the design will be provided to the staff responsible for developing the infrastructure, and the cloud providers will be contacted to determine the size, cost, and storage. Also, in this phase, testing of the virtual community will be conducted and maybe even that of a pilot used to determine the efficiency of the community.

(3) In the "Check" phase, the evaluation of the community will be examined to determine whether what was planned and developed is actually

working. Corrections may be noted and logged in order to rework specific areas that failed.

(4) In the "Act" phase, a determination will be made as to whether the virtual community is working effectively with the cloud technology. Also, it would be important to evaluate whether the overall process is working fine and if changes need to be made before putting the community in place.

After using the PDCA process, it can be determined whether the community is ready to use an effective approach to managing students in the community. Staffing and support are critical areas for a virtual community project. There needs to be an evaluation of the process, and a decision needs to be made as to whether staff members need support and training before moving forward with the virtual community project.

After the community is developed and the structure has been put into place, staff can begin logging the students in and out and providing them with indiviudal user names and passwords. Guidelines for passwords and user names need to be established. Teachers will also need to be given rights to access the site and may also be given some administrative rights to manage student activities and access.

Training is a critical part of the process and if teachers want to use the community as an additional resource for their classroom, they need to go through specific administrative training. Areas of teacher training may include: logging into the system, managing passwords, providing specific access rights to different individuals, and reporting problems and errors with the system. The effectiveness of the virtual community will depend on how the teachers manage the course and curriculum as well as the assessment of the students. So a decision needs to be made by the teacher to determine whether the virtual community is useful and will be manageable as part of the teaching process for the students. If the project of the virtual community progresses so will the planning of the virtual community and the type of cloud technology that is needed. The cloud technology may hold the key to success of the virtual community and that is why it is necessary to understand how the setup works and how the cloud environment will be planned out.

CLOUD TECHNOLOGY

The environment that is created using cloud technology will be an important part of the development of the virtual community. Not only the cloud technology will impact the virtual community but it will also be the catalyst for collaborating and managing the community. In order to understand how far our technology has grown, it is important to understand some part of the history that brought the Internet to the point it is today.

As Jabbour (2013) noted, the Internet has progressed and developed over the years. From early 1990 to 2000, there has been a continual development of the Internet, providing information to its users. Web 1.0 was the first development of the Internet. Then with Web 2.0 in 2006, the web took on a different form introducing web applications. As technology continues to expand, with the introduction of Web 3.0, not only technology will improve but also more ways for individuals to interact through social networking will be introduced.

It is interesting to note how progressive technology has been and how it has progressed from Web 1.0 to Web 3.0. This development over time from basic Internet usage that included basic HTML pages, forms, and views has move to blogs and the ability to share content using XML (Jabbour, 2013). This movement from basic HTML and basic web interfaces to blogs and extensive HTML has improved the way we view information on the Internet. Figure 3 illustrates the interaction between different environments, showing the main virtual environment and its association with Wikis, blogs, and podcasts.

Figure 3. Virtual Environment and Different Areas

Since technology has increased in different ways to present and communicate information, it has opened the door for security issues. As technology continues to progress, looking at methods to secure information is necessary. It is important that schools continually evaluate different approaches to securing their data. This is also important for the virtual learning community.

Important parts of security are policies and procedures that should be evaluated on a continual basis as changes occur. Setting up policies and procedures is necessary in order to maintain control and authorized access to a school's information. This is also an important area for the virtual community. As noted by Divya and Parakasam (2015), three critical areas need to be accounted for when securing cloud information and data. There needs to be a way to keep information confidential, there needs to be a way to maintain the accuracy of information, and there needs to be a way to access and use information. Keeping information confidential is part of the Privacy Act. The Privacy Act of 1974 was put into place to protect records of names, social security numbers, and other numbers that may be used to identify individuals. Also, the Act was used to prohibit the disclosure of records without a written consent. This privacy Act binds Federal agencies and covers records for them.

There is also the E-Government Act of 2002 that makes governmental agencies keep personal information private. The HHS.gov website provides additional information on specific privacy laws and will be useful when determining how to secure information that may be personally identifiable (HHS.gov, 2016). The accuracy of information is critical and there needs to be a plan in place for checking and performing the quality assurance of it. It would be useful for a quality analyst to develop a process and then use the same process for working through a methodical approach to evaluating the information that is for the virtual community.

A checklist would be a good way to set up a listing to manage the data and information. As the quality assurance analyst goes through specific checks s/he can note areas that need correction and improvement. Information needs to be easy to access so that staff and teachers can manage, continually improve, and keep that up to date. All three areas play a critical role in developing an environment that is secure while maintaining the integrity and accuracy of information. The users that access the information need to know that the information is valid, secure, and can be accessed when they need it. Managing the accuracy, validity, and control over the data is part of keeping the virtual community success-ful, reliable and valid. The next section provides information on how the cloud community and the virtual community work together to form a working environment.

THE CLOUD AND THE COMMUNITY

The key to development of an effective cloud community is to make sure that there is up-to-date technology, the ability to secure information, and a way to house and archive the information. One of the most im-portant aspects of cloud computing is its development that creates an environment using different aspects of technology. Mousannif, Khalil, and Kotsis suggested that there are various concepts of cloud technology that include "virtualization technologies, Web services, service-oriented architecture (SOA), and distributed computing" (Mousannif, Khalil, & Kotsis, 2013, p. 159). Virtualization can be used as a way to limit space as well as the ability to operate and function in a multiple usage state. If various locations are set up, this may be referred to as multiple locations or virtual machines that all operate the same (Mousannif et al., 2013, p. 159). If different locations are set up, then the cloud environment can be managed through different virtual communities, however, all locations can use the same copy or image.

An understanding of how the cloud works, how information is used and stored, how services are provided to users, and how information is se-cured is important to understand about the cloud environment. It is also important to have an understanding of the basic architecture of the cloud environment. This understanding can help when troubleshooting areas that are not working and need attention.

There are three service models that are a part of cloud services that in-clude Software-as-a-Service (SaaS), Platform-as-a-Service (PaaS), and Infrastructure-as-a-Service (IaaS). Services may include email and appli-cations that are virtual and web services. According to Mousannif et al., "The SOA facilitates interoperable services between distributed systems to communicate and exchange data with one another, thus providing a uniform means for service users and providers to discover and offer services respectively" (Mousannif et al., 2013, p. 160). SOA is a service used in the development of a cloud environment. Through these environments, a sharing of information and exchanging data provides service for the users.

Sharing of information and understanding how much space is necessary may impact the type of software that is needed for the cloud. Schools can make good use of the cloud computing environment by providing students the software package they need as well as setting up special services such as emails and systems in the cloud environment. The setup provides users with the ability to utilize the service at most any location and can cut down on the need for specialized software that students may need on an individual basis. So costs are cut and the systems can operate quickly while versions are kept up to date on the cloud based on the agreed upon software package and services from the service provider. As students move from class to class and keeping the cloud up to date, different software is required. As budgets become tighter and tighter, different ways of helping students find more affordable opportunities will make using the cloud and the cloud community more cost-effective to students (Mousannif et al., 2013, p. 161). The cloud environment can be managed and be cost-effective using different services based on the service provider, curriculum development that utilizes different software, and virtual community requirements for specific software.

An example of cloud computing services may be Google, Amazon, Salesforce.com, and Microsoft (Thomas, 2011, p. 4). Since there are many different cloud services available, it is important to carefully evaluate what each service offers and at which price. The provider may offer many different services that can be used to accommodate different areas for the virtual community. The virtual community may be considered a "Virtual Learning Environment" or a "Personal Learning Environment" (Thomas, 2011, p. 5). These environments are developed based on the needs of the environment, the user of the environment, why will the environment be used, when will the environment be used, and when will access be provided to users.

Through the setup of virtual and personal learning environments, students can not only connect with their teachers and classmates but they can also connect with other school students and teachers depending on how the environment is structured and how access and rights are given to other virtual communities. This opens the door for sharing information and data that can help students not only increase knowledge but also expand their networking to other schools.

As students begin sharing information and networking with other schools, it will be necessary to continually evaluate the cloud environment to make sure that it provides the access to different servers and connections. According to Thomas, "This network of servers and connections is collectively known as the cloud. Physically, the resource may sit on a bunch of servers at different data centres or even span across continents" (Thomas, 2011, p. 4). Since a network spans over many different locations or networks, this increases the availability of services. This can be very advantageous as it reduces the need for schools and virtual communities to have their own networking services and data centers. So if schools cannot afford to have large servers, networks, or human capital to run the data center, they may be able to establish the network with other schools.

This is particularly useful for colleges and universities that have limited resources and budget for technology. As Thomas (2011) noted, the cloud environment can be useful for evaluating a working environment and is convenient for teaching. Being convenient is also a part of the advantage of storing information in the cloud without the need of storage drives. Using multiple locations with the cloud can be advantageous as well as useful for students and teachers that may go to various locations for studying and teaching. Also, the processing of the information using the cloud can be quicker and more efficient because of its larger capacity to handle a large amount of data (Thomas, 2011).

Understanding the cloud environment will be beneficial when setting up virtual communities. If the environment is set up properly, then there is an advantage of developing virtual communities that can reach a large number of individuals. A working environment can help to expand the community and work toward achieving the goals of spreading a large amount of information and data throughout the community. In the next chapter, there will be a discussion on the advantages of developing e-collaboration through virtual communities using cloud technology.

CHAPTER 2.
ADVANTAGES DEVELOPING A VIRTUAL
COMMUNITY USING CLOUD TECHNOLOGY

IMPORTANCE OF VIRTUAL COMMUNITIES

Developing and managing a virtual community has its challenges. However, a virtual community can also have many advantages. One of the biggest advantages of a virtual community is that it can open the door for communication via e-collaboration that is paramount. The key is to set up the virtual community in a way that allows individuals with the same interests, ideas, and information to collaborate as well as share and engage in conversations that will expand knowledge, skills, and abilities. This can be pivotal for the e-learning environment, as this form of collaboration can be held outside of the classroom at a time convenient to all participants.

Virtual communities can be useful for modernizing the delivery of content as well as promoting individualized student centered learning. As noted in Chapter 1, the cloud computing environment architecture includes: Platform as a Service (PaaS), Software as a service (SaaS), and Infrastructure as a Service (IaaS). A discussion was presented describing how PaaS is an important part of the architecture necessary for programs. SaaS or software as a service is needed so that users can access software in the cloud, and IaaS or the infrastructure as a service is the model for the basis of cloud computing infrastructure (Isaila, 2014).

When discussing the advantages of cloud computing, Isaila suggested that "the biggest advantage is related to the low cost and use learning content anytime and anywhere. Learning material is easily maintained and updated; it may include multimedia content to facilitate understanding of concepts" (Isaila 2014, p. 100). Providing cost savings not only to schools but also to the students is a big plus. This cost savings is advantageous for schools because of limited budgets. As colleges and universities continue to look for ways to minimize spending and increase services, it would be advantageous to consider the use of cloud computing.

Cloud computing provides users with different ways to utilize multimedia that may otherwise not be considered as a means of communication. It is advantageous to consider how software applications that can be costly to the school and students can be a part of cloud technology, thereby minimizing the continual updates of software, patches, or upgrades. The setup of the virtual community should be evaluated by assessing the goals and objectives as well as the needs of the community.

COMMUNITY SETUP

The virtual community setup can be an easy process if schools or universities have providers who can work with them while addressing the specific goals and objectives laid out for the virtual community. Meeting with a cloud provider will ensure that a discussion about specific services that are needed are also aligned with the virtual community's goals and objectives.

The setup of the virtual community may involve individual groups, cloud technology specialists, software tool engineers, and networking technologists. Each group of individuals will be able to provide specific input beneficial to the selection of a service provider that offers the best services. The group needs to be able to evaluate specific features that are necessary and are the most beneficial while impacting the strength of communication and the management of the community. The group needs to concentrate on the selection of the cloud service and this should be a focused effort with reliance on expertise and experience.

Examples of different cloud computing services are iCloud, Egnyte, Google Apps, OpenDrive, Dropbox, and Amazon Cloud Drive. Each of the aforementioned offers services that the virtual community would find helpful in meeting their goals. Some of the services provided by the different cloud computing service providers are email usage, calendars, documents, spreadsheets, file storage, file encryption, mobile access using iPhone, iPad, or the android. When evaluating providers, support is also an important area to consider, and it is important to see if the service provider charges for support or if this is part of the service package.

An example of a review is with Amazon Cloud Drive. This service provider indicated that for $1.66 (prices subject to change), it is possible to obtain tiered storage plans; however, there is no file sharing or mobile access. The service is limited to web browsers and devices that are compatible with Adobe. This can be a drawback if the virtual community has users that access the virtual community using mobile devices (Purch, 2016).

Another cloud service provider is Goggle Apps by Google. This service offers users the ability to store content using any device as long as there is an Internet connection for $5.00 a month (prices subject to change). A drawback to the use of Google Apps is that in order to use content there may be a different app for specific content usage. Also, there is a limitation on the type of interface or access to a portal for the apps (Google, 2016). The method in which information is shared based on the cloud service will impact which learning management system (LMS) is selected for the virtual community.

By evaluating different options of cloud-based LMSs, teachers and staff can select the best platform that meets the most criteria for the virtual community. Pappas (2013) suggested 20 different cloud-based LMSs that could be evaluated to determine whether the service would be useful for the virtual community. These systems have different options and features that make each service unique.

Following is a list that Pappas (2013) developed for cloud-based learning management systems:

- Talent LMS
- Docebo SaaS LMS by Docebo
- Litmos LMS by Litmos
- Administrate
- WiZDOM LMS by G-Cube
- Mindflash Online Training LMS by Mindflash
- Latitude Learning LMS by Latitude Learning
- Inquisiq R3 LMS by ICS Learning Group

- Haiku LMS by Haiku Learning Systems
- Luminosity LMS by CM-Group
- Integrated LMS by Integrated LMS
- Skillport LMS by Skillsoft
- Scholar LMS by vTraining Room
- eLearning247 LMS by eLearning247
- ExpertusONE Cloud LMS by Expertus
- Joule LMS by Moodlerooms
- 30 hands Cloud by 30 hands Learning
- VTA Talent Management Suite by RISC Inc.
- Learning Evolution by Learning Evolution

The aforementioned systems all have specific and unique services that are specific for their organization and can be evaluated based on the community's goals and objectives. A college or university can try different virtual platforms on a trial basis and can set up a checklist to evaluate the different platforms. The checklist may include the following criteria: security, content, cost, features, interface, usability, accessibility, upgrades, maintenance, support, user licenses, can this run on the cloud, self-design, translation feature, and a grading criteria of scale 1–3; 1—Dislike—2—Possible—3—Like.

The checklist can be used by teachers, staff, and students to evaluate each area and a comparison can be made to help evaluate each specific criterion. An example of this checklist for various platforms is shown in Table 1.

Table 1. Checklist for Platforms

Platform	Teacher	Staff	Student
1. Security			
2. Content			
3. Cost			
4. Features			
5. Interface			
6. Usability			
7. Accessibility			
8. Upgrades			
9. Maintenance			
10. Support			
11. User Licenses			
12. Run on Cloud			
13. Self-Design			
14. Translation feature			

Legend—Scale 1-3—1—Dislike—2—Possible—3—Like

Looking at various virtual learning platforms will take time so it is important to set up a timeline for evaluating different LMS. Since there are so many different LMSs, selecting several to get an idea of the different features would be a good first step. An example of an LMS reviewed is Joule LMS.

Joule LMS can be downloaded and tested for free (Moodlerooms, 2012). This LMS platform offers tools that can support the content and activities for those in virtual environments. Progress can be tracked and individualized instruction can be provided. This platform provides support and can be combined with Moodlerooms which is an open-source platform. The 15-day free trial is useful for evaluating the platform to make sure that it meets the needs of the students and staff.

Using the checklist aforementioned, it is possible not only to receive feedback from students, staff, and teachers but also to compare the different features with other platforms before purchasing the application or securing the software package on the cloud. A key feature of the platform includes an open-source platform that Moodlerooms offer. Open-source software makes its code available to change and update to meet the needs of the users. The platform is easy to use and create, and it provides quality to the users who access the cloud environment. The performance of individuals in the community can be monitored and even personalized as well as graded. Reports can be produced and used to evaluate the community's activity and progress. Pricing can be evaluated based on the block of storage, services used, training, and other additional features that may be necessary for the community.

Another review of a virtual LMS is called Integrated LMS (2012). This platform is considered an integrated platform because of its ability to interact with other systems. This LMS is useful for storing student information on a cloud-based platform. This platform provides an integrated approach to the storage of information and can be integrated as an admission management system as well as an LMS.

This platform is considered useful for higher education and its approach to managing different aspects of a student's individual needs such as registering, paying, and even the use of the virtual library. Since Integrated LMS focuses on an individual student, it would be beneficial in managing individual participants for a virtual learning community. This system partners with Salesforce.com and can be downloaded from the AppExchange and accessed free for 21 days. This cloud application is considered an SaaS program that can be used to manage admissions, virtual classes using a Moodle learning system, and provide virtual collaboration and communication as a part of Adobe Connect.

In addition to the aforementioned LMSs by Pappas (2013), Durand (2011) also noted that different virtual community platforms are available that can be used for collaboration and sharing information. Some of these platforms were also a part of the listing mentioned earlier. However, there are additional platforms as well to consider. Each of the following provides a unique feature for developing and maintaining a virtual community platform in a virtual environment:

- Drupal
- Get Satisfaction
- Jive
- Joomla
- Kickapp
- Mzinga
- Ning

- PHP-Nuke
- Pligg
- Telligent
- Episerver Relate
- Social Engine
- BuddyPress
- IGLOO

For example, in the aforementioned list, there is Drupal that is a learning management platform that can be utilized for content management. Drupal has many features relative to content management that includes "content authoring, reliable performance, and excellent security" (Drupal, para 1). Drupal is open-source software and can be retrieved and downloaded to use and share, change and modify to suit the needs of the users. This software is considered "built on principles like collaboration, globalism, and innovation" (Drupal, para 3). This concept is important since the virtual community can be accessed on a globalized manner to achieve collaboration that promotes innovation.

Another example is—Get Satisfaction—which is another virtual community useful for individuals who want to meet and work together. This platform is useful for developing virtual company–customer relationships. The advantage of this platform is to provide a quick way to interact with other customers. Its expertise in the virtual platform can be used to provide a cohesive interaction among members. This platform is also considered a virtual customer community that can build on relationships with those who have common interests and want feedback on different purchases (Get Satisfaction, 2014). Although the focus is based on building purchasing relationships and sharing purchasing information, this platform is a form of a virtual community where individuals meet to exchange ideas and information. This virtual community platform may be used to meet and exchange information as well as develop virtual community purchasing relationships that may apply to educational supplies. The Get Satisfaction platform is useful in maintaining a virtual customer community and is used to share expertise between customers in the community. This platform offers those who are the part of the community the ability to interact and have conversations with others who share the same educational interest.

Pligg CMS is a platform that can be used to create a virtual community. This LMS can be used to manage virtual content as well as to provide individuals the ability to contribute to a virtual community. With this platform, content can be developed and used by individuals participating in the community. The Pligg CMS platform also provides the groups the capability of developing and managing as well as it helps develop member profiles, which can show various interests between members. Pligg CMS also offers a search engine for its members to look for those with similar interests. The Pligg CMS platform is an open-source software platform that can be used and managed by programmers. Modules can be set up and developed using templates to manage the code design. Because of the global impact of the virtual learning community, an important feature of this open-source software is that it offers 12 different languages (Pligg LLC, 2016).

The Joomla platform is another useful platform for a virtual LMS. In Figure 1, the illustration provides a basic interface showing the various features for the Joomla learning management platform. The Joomla platform is an open-source multilingual platform that is offered in 64 languages. There are many ways that 7000 extensions can be used to expand and extend its platform. The content management system advantage of Joomla provides many different features useful in managing the community and content. The front end can be managed, edited, and changed because it is open-source software. One of the biggest advantages of the Joomla platform is its ability to manage the content with no technical skill needed. This can be beneficial to schools since funding may be limited for finding specific skill sets to manage and deploy the virtual LMS. Companies and businesses have made use of the open-source software platform and have easily developed and manage the Joomla platform (Open Source Matters, 2016).

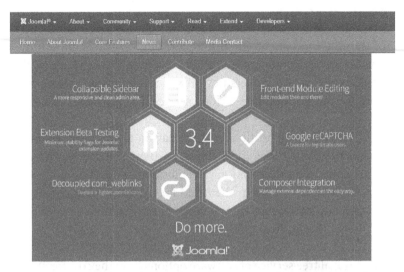

Figure 1. Features of Joomla (Joomla—Release 3.4.2—(https://www.joomla.org/announcements/release-news/5589-joomla-3-4-2-released.html).

Joomla offers features that are unique for their system that includes a collapsible sidebar for administrative usage. Joomla also offers beta testing to determine extensions that are useful for managing updates. There are also decoupled com web links. Front-end module editing provides for a front-end approach to editing modules. Also, there are Google reCAPTCHA that provides for legitimate users and a composer integration for managing external dependencies.

Each of the aforementioned platforms and tools is central to understanding features and how the different features can be applied to the specific needs of a virtual learning community. Carefully evaluating the various platforms by appraising free demos will be a useful approach to determining which platform will have the biggest impact on the virtual learning community. Many platforms have demos that can be downloaded for free, which is a cost savings for the school. Service providers may also include learning tools as part of their service. An evaluation of the different tools may help in determining the best platform for the virtual community.

LEARNING TOOLS

Since learning tools are an important part of the virtual community, an evaluation process would be useful. Microsoft and Google are available to provide colleges and universities with educational applications as part of a free service. For example, a cloud service may provide:

> "... free office applications without having to purchase, install and maintain these applications on their computers; there are enhanced collaboration possibilities; their data do not get lost, these are stored in the cloud for free use and accessible from any location or from a range of devices such as mobile phone" (Isaila, 2014, p. 101).

This additional free service of software options frays the cost for students as well as decreases an added expense of required software for students. This free service along with application storage can be an advantage and help in determining the correct service provider for the virtual community. Application storage can take up considerable space on the school servers. The evaluation of additional storage as part of the service can help in determining which cloud provider provides the best storage capability for the school. Isaila (2014) also noted that educational institutions need to take advantage of how the development of cloud computing impacts resources such as hardware, software, resources, and services that are provided to the community. These services are critical and become apparent when setting up the community and collaborating and sharing information.

COLLABORATION AND SHARING IDEAS

Cloud services can be valuable to an educational organization that goes beyond the storage of data, increasing performance, and managing software. Additional strategic areas that are important as noted in Figure 2 are considerations that Isaila (2014) suggested:

- Cost savings
- Increased performance
- No need for updating software

- Availability of documents for students
- Availability for teachers
- Technical support is available but may be a part of the cloud providers
- Security and confidential areas to monitor

Since colleges and universities are continually looking for ways to save money, cloud computing can be used to increase educational performance while managing costs. Schools can save money because they do not need to constantly update and keep track of software and students can save money because they can utilize software that has been stored on the cloud. Schools can work with the cloud service providers when students and staff need new or additional software and as curriculum changes. Also, schools can request technical support from the cloud service provider, which is important for managing technical issues that occur which may include security issues.

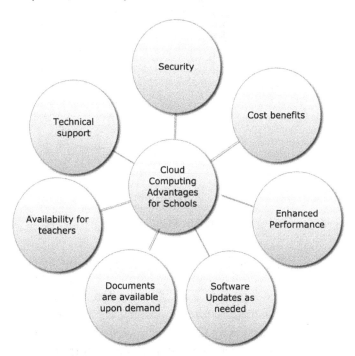

Figure 2. Cloud Computing Advantages for Schools

Minimizing costs and increasing performance are all part of any schools goals and objectives. This can also be part of a cost-saving program. Cost-effective education will increase schools' effectiveness and even help in retention. Since schools are constantly looking for ways to improve and increase their approach to learning, selecting the right providers and platforms is necessary. As noted in Figure 3, it is important to establish guidelines that can be used to manage a working effort between teachers, staff, and students. Both cloud computing and communities of learning are ways to increase the interaction between students and staff while sharing information and fostering virtual interaction.

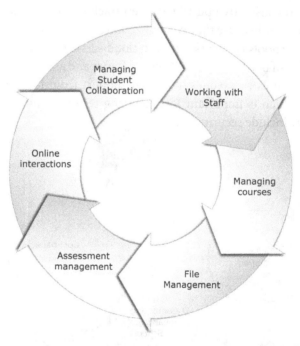

Figure 3. Cloud Based E-Learning

The growth of the Internet has led to the increase in the diversification of the web, virtual technology, and e-collaboration. The growth of technology has provided a positive impact on the communication process, particularly how students and teachers interact through social media. As noted by Divya and Prakasam (2015), technology continues to progress, and colleges and universities are working toward incorporating technology into the delivery of their materials, information, and assessments. Cloud technology has helped to increase the storage of information and has become beneficial to schools because of the decrease of storage on a school server. The cloud can increase the availability and location of materials for students and teachers that will lead to an increase in their performance as well as lowering the costs for students. As the cost of services decreases, the impact of services to the student's increases and this provides a better learning environment.

Since e-learning can be dynamic and ever changing, colleges and universities need to recognize that the cloud e-learning environment and the role the environment plays in the traditional face-to-face environment are necessary. This not only applies to a virtual classroom but also to the traditional face-to-face environment. The traditional classroom can make use of the virtual community because of the diverse usage the virtual environment offers to teachers and students. The traditional classroom can have a blended environment that consists of the traditional face-to-face environment along with a virtual platform that offers extended virtual learning options.

Divya and Parakasam (2015) noted that the architecture of the cloud-based e-learning system can have many different functioning parts that include virtual labs, discussion boards, virtual course rooms, resources for instructors, and administrative functions. Teachers who work in a face-to-face traditional educational environment can make use of the virtual community as an extension of the classroom and look at whether virtual labs, virtual course rooms, and additional discussion forums can enhance the traditional curriculum.

That is why it is important that traditional teachers work with virtual teachers to exchange information to determine how the virtual learning community can be used for both environments. Virtual teachers and face-to-face teachers can set up a virtual learning community to share different techniques in the virtual learning community. As you can see, the environment can be expanded not only for students and teachers but also for teachers who want to discuss virtual techniques with other teachers. Teachers should discuss the importance of how the environment can be used and how the environment needs to be secured where other teachers can learn different techniques that may be useful for their classrooms. Information security can be managed by both virtual instructors and traditional classroom teachers. Securing information is important since there may be such information as testing materials and grades that need to be kept confidential.

Securing information on the cloud is what educators are concerned about and want to address so that the information is not compromised. As per Divya and Prakasam, "Information security depends on the three principles of confidentiality (who has access), integrity (correctness of information), and availability (ability to access information and services at appropriate times)" (Divya & Prakasam, 2015, p. 31). Maintaining confidentiality, keeping integrity, and having the information available are areas to consider when managing software and should be a part of the training process for staff and teachers. Students and teachers need to have the assurance that when they post information on a virtual environment, there is a method in place to keep the confidentiality and the integrity of the information while making the information available when needed.

Security and management policies should be reviewed and updated on a continuous basis. This may be a challenge for the cloud community. As Divya and Prakasam noted, "When data and services reside on servers, external to the campus, however, safeguarding those assets involves additional concerns. Encrypting data in transit is important, as are the service provider's security procedures" (Divya & Prakasam, 2015, p. 31). This statement addresses the need for a process of securing information by establishing procedures with the help of encrypting passwords, log-ons, and personal data to ensure that the information is confidential, particularly in the case of the cloud environment.

After evaluating the security needs, teachers will have the confidence that no matter if the community is a virtual community or a face-to-face classroom, there are specific standards and guidelines developed to ensure security. The security needs are useful guidelines that will help while setting up specific areas in the virtual community, including a community focused on specific information for smaller groups or modules.

Different modules within the community are considered groups or a small copy of the main virtual environment. Using groups can be advantageous as this can increase the interaction between those who share information and resources that may relate to an extended study of a topic. For example, if a class is studying the importance of social media for collaboration, separate groups on the topic can be set up, and each group could explore an aspect of social media, such as Wikis, blogs, and podcasts, and each provides research and information on each form of social media to share with the main environment.

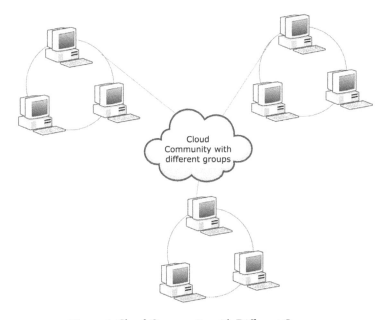

Figure 4. Cloud Community with Different Groups.

Figure 4 provides a representation of how groups may be set up and how the interaction in the cloud community using groups may work. The development of the groups is one way to increase the interaction between teachers and students. The use of this technique can increase the interaction between students, teachers, and other classes. There can be an exchange of information that can be used to further the existing topic and then utilized in another class or virtual community for further research. In the next chapter, there will be a discussion on the challenges of developing an e-collaborative virtual community using cloud technology.

CHAPTER 3.
CHALLENGES DEVELOPING A VIRTUAL
COMMUNITY USING CLOUD TECHNOLOGY

CHALLENGES OF A VIRTUAL COMMUNITY

Challenges are the part of any project and can also be the part of a virtual community. Some challenges may include identifying and working with a cloud provider, establishing a direction for the virtual community, selecting software to use on the cloud and keeping participants active in the virtual community. Problems in the development of the virtual community can inhibit the future development and growth of the community. Also, specific drawbacks like the lack of budgeting could negatively impact the forward progress of the virtual community.

Dillon, Wu, and Chang (2010) noted different issues and challenges that can negatively impact the advancement of cloud computing and e-learning. Several examples include the security of information, data, performance, availability, and difficulty integrating the cloud services with current applications that will impact cost. Not only security can be one of the biggest issues but maintaining and managing data and files can also be a big challenge. Since different individuals will have access to the files and data, it is imperative that there be security guidelines be in place for managing the data and the information. As new individuals enter the community and different teachers manage the virtual community, continual training efforts need to be put in place. The training should consist of data management, security policies, and internal operations. This along with understanding the assessment and evaluation of individuals in the community will be useful when management evaluates the performance and success of the virtual community.

Since performance and availability are ongoing concerns, the impact needs to be evaluated as to whether the virtual community can operate and manage collaboration and participation on demand. As the virtual community grows, so will the demands of space and availability.

As Dillon et al. (2010) noted, the management of the data may involve complex data structures that are used by the cloud SaaS (Software as a Service) and this may increase the need for the integration of different services outsourced to different service vendors. This can work into areas where management needs to assess the drawbacks that may occur for developing the virtual community.

It is important to note that drawbacks for developing a virtual community can be turned into advantages. This can occur by managing the services that impact the community in a positive way. The impact of using the cloud for the virtual community includes understanding how different applications such as computer, mobile phones, and tablets interact, perform, and function when accessing the cloud.

Evaluating performance is necessary, and as the community changes and grows, there may be a need to reevaluate the requirements to determine whether processes increase performance or decrease performance. Performance improves with the use of a cloud provider because the school does not have to focus on software that minimizes the continual use of updates and patches that cloud providers maintain. If software is kept up to date by cloud providers, files and data are readily available and accessed upon demand. The staff may do quality checks instead of software installation, which improves efficiency and effectiveness of the virtual community that puts less demand on the in-house servers and staff.

Individuals who are the part of the virtual community need to make a commitment not only to other individuals in the community but to themselves. Scheduling should be realistic and meet the required deadlines for the community and extended classwork, so that when projects and assignments are due, it can be accomplished. Since the virtual community brings together not only individuals who share the same interest, there may also be others who share a common interest in the group. Scheduling should be set up to accommodate all individuals who may be a part of the community. Managing group dynamics encourages others to maintain a professional demeanor and also encourages others to participate in the virtual community (Raudenbush, 2016).

Zhao and Kuh (2004) noted that there are different purposes for the virtual community. An example may be that the community is used for curriculum evaluation or actual classroom training. Also, the virtual community can be useful for those living in residential learning environments and developed for students who want to learn a specific topic. The learning community provides an environment that can be structured to make a connection between students and specific topics. A connection between students can be used to open up a social network that can grow over time. This social network encourages a continual relationship between individuals that may endure even if the community ends.

As communication continues through social networking, it is noted that "text-based communication is inherently slower than spoken communication" (Trent, 2016, para 2). Although text-based communication is slower, it does have an advantage as it uses a written documentation that can be reviewed and reread if necessary. The social network is also useful for managing issues that instructors may have concerning access to the community, "In online education, instructors are available via e-mail, but they cannot be accessed directly through office hours" (Trent, 2016, para 3). This is critical in a virtual learning environment. Having access that is available 24/7 can be useful and accommodate students and teachers in an ongoing manner. Students and teachers can log on at any time, post their questions, comments, and answer questions that are posted. A communication process is beneficial for students, teachers, and staff in order to work toward a process that permits continual questions and feedback to the learning process.

Questions may be lost in email communication from students; however, the virtual community may be an effective way to manage a social networking where questions can be posted and answered in a discussion forum format. Providing a positive approach to communication while managing a positive interaction between users will help to increase the interaction and learning process. Students and teachers can be active participants, but there should be someone accountable for managing the community so that students and teachers do not feel that the virtual community is a waste of time and effort for communicating.

It is important to note that problems may occur with the peer interaction where "classrooms can lack a sense of community and lead to a feeling of isolation. They also reduce the opportunity to network with others, which can be a disadvantage as students finish school and begin to look for new work opportunities" (Trent, 2016, para 4). The key is to be available and schedule time virtually so that students know that someone is around to communicate with about specific areas of interest. Problems can occur when users do not actively communicate but rely on the teacher to carry out all the interaction and communication. This leads to an isolated environment. In this case, the teacher should set up time for virtual meetings where students who feel this isolation can meet and discuss topics of their interest and provide feedback to the teacher on different areas of the course.

It's not that all students feel isolated; they enjoy working on their own because of personal and professional obligations. The key is to provide the option and make the option available so that everyone has the benefit of a true virtual experience that may include a synchronous or an asynchronous experience. If meeting virtually would be beneficial, then time needs to be set aside to meet the virtual obligations of the virtual classroom and the virtual community. It is noted that time management and technology may impact the virtual classroom and the virtual community, but it should not be considered a disadvantage for communicating and completing assignments. Maybe the real culprit is procrastination and the lack of time management skills. If this is the issue, then an evaluation should be made as to why students are procrastinating and why they lack time management skills. It may be because they do not understand how to use the technology of the different platforms or they do not have the time to learn about the different platforms that the school is using. Since technology impacts the virtual community, keeping up with current technology is necessary. Even though there may be a lack of funding, issues in gaining access to the classroom, and meeting deadlines, technological issues need to be addressed and solved if the community is to be successful (Trent, 2016, para 5 and 6). It is important to see how technology greatly impacts the success of a community as well as impact the success of students.

Charalambos and Michalinos (2004) noted, "Online communities face several challenges among which some are technological and some social. The technological component relates to the continuous development and improvement of tools that will allow participants to utilize them without a steep learning curve" (Charalambos & Michalinos, 2004, p. 137). Training should be offered so that everyone who uses the virtual community feels comfortable with the technology and is able to easily access the community and work in the community unencumbered. Training questions about the different platforms should be a part of the evaluation. Also, the training should be delivered in a way that all students, staff and teachers can easily access the materials and gain knowledge without additional training.

Technological changes may also impact the use of the cloud service provider who can help keep the schools technically up to date with software as well as minimize the use of maintenance for software applications. The cloud service provider has a responsibility to keep a higher level of security and manage the data and technology in a manner that is confidential and protected (Isaila, 2014). Figure 1 provides an illustration of how different considerations are a part of cloud technology. Cost, security, availability/performance, and management of data/integration of services are all important considerations for understanding cloud technology. The mentioned areas are important for understanding when it is time to make improvements and monitor the virtual community.

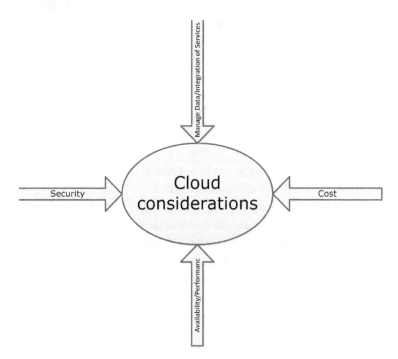

Figure 1. Cloud Considerations

MONITORING THE VIRTUAL COMMUNITY

Monitoring a virtual community is essential for determining whether the activities in the community are making progress. Glassmeyer, Dibbs, and Jensen discussed how students feel about the virtual environment and when students were queried about what they felt was important for virtual communication: "Students frequently brought up virtual community in their responses. Students mentioned feelings of connecting and communicating were vital to their online education experience, especially sharing perspectives with one another" (Glassmeyer, Dibbs, & Jensen, 2011, p. 28). That feeling of joining and communicating on a level outside the virtual classroom brings about a connectedness beneficial for students and teachers. This connectedness can be beneficial for completing and engaging in additional activities outside the classroom. Through continual engagement and collaborative interaction there can be an increase in knowledge for specific areas that can be used to establish educational relationships and support a mentoring environment.

Monitoring the virtual community also means keeping information up to date and archived when necessary. Anderson et al. discussed how "archival educators are increasingly challenged to find methods of teaching about digital objects and records that reflect the global virtual environments in which these records are created and reside" (Anderson et al., 2011, p. 350). The expansion of the virtual community will create the need for file management and this demand will continue to grow as the community grows. This is where cloud computing can become advantageous and supportive for the virtual learning community. The key is to have a plan for managing an archive system. For example, the archive system may take the form of a database, data warehouse, or a data mart. A system or method of housing the data and information needs to be set up and available that is useful for the virtual community. Staff may be responsible for managing this activity and advise students and teachers how to access and retrieve archived data. As the data are stored, students should have access to the information as it is needed. The availability of information provides students the comfort of knowing that, when they access the virtual community, information on specific topics is available for their use.

The virtual community can also be used as a learning tool for understanding complex simulated real-world scenarios. Anderson et al. discussed how a virtual lab is "an educational tool, an immediate concern is with the educational environment itself, with creating a learning space that students can trust, and where they, as a community, can work in assured and comfortable relationships" (Anderson et al. 2011, p., 358). The work that the students create in the virtual lab needs to be reliable and provide valid real world results. The creation of an environment that is secure will make the information valid and reliable. The trust that is established in the environment can help students "be confident that the systems they are using are authentic, even though they may be demonstration versions, and that the content in those systems is representative of real archival records and collections" (Anderson et al., 2011, p. 359). This virtual environment can be used to simulate how work may be used in real-world situations as well as how information is collected and archived for future use.

Developing an authentic environment increases a reliable archive collection of information. The collection of data and information may be large or small but needs to be monitored, managed, and controlled. Staff should be trained to monitor and manage the archives for students and teachers. According to Anderson et al., "As every educator knows, creating trust in a classroom environment is a complex web of diverse elements embracing social relationships among students and between students and instructors" (Anderson et al., 2011, p. 358). As relationships are developed in the virtual classroom, trust is developed and this will carry over to future classes. Relationship building impacts the virtual community and can be used for future course curriculum development as well as developing a community and positive interaction between teachers, students, and staff.

Community building can be "related to cognitive style and the way that individuals learn, so that the instructional design of an online learning environment is also a key component in the ability of the participants to form a community" (Anderson et al., 2011, p. 359). The sense of community drives the virtual community forward as it creates a collaborative and cohesive impact between its members. Virtual community building for the students can provide an interaction with others who may have similar learning styles. As students work together in their community, they can share their interests, skills, and knowledge. The community may take on a style that is unique for it. This can provide the community with a distinctive value that would relate to a perceptive approach for it.

Monitoring the virtual community is necessary and important; therefore, some additional considerations should be evaluated. As suggested, the virtual community is a good source of information for students who want to learn not only about their environment but also about other learning environments. Teachers can monitor various groups of students who meet in the virtual community and match students with similar interests to other students on a local, regional, national, or even a global basis. It is noted that "creating an online learning community will facilitate a community of practice involving students from widely different cultural and social milieus" (Anderson et al., 2011, p. 359). This widely created culture will improve the diversity of the virtual community group and broaden the values and interests of those in the group. The globalization of the virtual community can impact the learning potential of everyone in the community. This widely created group of individuals will be able to access information and meet with others through discussions and exchange of information, which will create a multicultural exchange of ideas and knowledge. Therefore, it is important to have a plan for keeping the virtual community up to date.

KEEPING THE VIRTUAL COMMUNITY UP TO DATE TO INCREASE PARTICIPATION

Information needs to be accurate, reliable, and valid. Therefore, it is necessary to have checks and balances in place. The ability to manage information and keep accurate records will be paramount as the community grows. The validity of the information will provide reliable results as students and teachers access and use the information. In order to keep the virtual community up to date, it is essential to have a way to run checks on the information and monitor this on a regular basis. Since a database can be a useful tool for archiving and housing data and information, reliable checking of the accuracy and validation of the database is needed. Setting up a regular schedule to validate and retrieve information as a form of testing data should be done. Periodic scheduling and testing should be done to validate the information. Keeping up with the current information will increase the benefits of knowledge sharing, the number of participants in the community, and knowledge sharing.

Knowledge sharing that occurs in a virtual community may impact a social exchange relationship based on the social exchange theory. This theory suggests that relationships are determined and created among others
depending on the topic. This form of relationship development can increase information sharing and help the community grow. Through relationship development, knowledge is shared and learning occurs. If the
social exchange relationship increases so will the motivation to continue
to be a part of the community. Also, if the information is useful and helps
students improve and excel in their classes, they will be motivated by
those in the community to continue, which will increase growth in the
community (Chen, Fan, & Tsai, 2014).

The virtual community does not need to be a costly effort and can be
achieved by completing an evaluation of different platforms as suggested
in Chapter 2. The evaluation can be completed using product demos that
simulate the real virtual environment. Students, teachers, and staff can
all participate and provide their feedback on the different platforms. If
budgeting does not permit the development of a virtual learning community, there are free virtual community groups that are set up and that
may provide the information needed.

Examples of free virtual learning communities are language communities, communities on civic learning, communities on science, communities for teachers, and general virtual learning communities. For example, there is a language community that is a free community entitled
Livemocha, Inc. where individuals come together to learn a language.
There are free lessons and chats that encourage individuals to speak the
language of choice.

Other examples of free virtual communities are education-related learning communities, such as TeacherTube, We The Teachers, and TeachAde.
Each of these communities provides information, shares videos, shares
resources, and even provides a social network for teachers (LearningPath.
org, 2016, para 1–5).

Table 1 provides names of different communities and their specific interests that may be useful when looking for a free virtual community to join.

Each community has a specific interest and is associated with specific topics related to a community interest. The interest ranges from language, environmental concerns, scientific interests, teachers, to miscellaneous groups. These examples show that there are many different virtual communities and many different areas of interest that are available to join. Communities exhibit appropriate guidelines for members who need to understand that the community is developed to provide a united effort on the topics. It is important to understand that, although the communities are free, to join them a professional demeanor is required.

Language-learning communities	
• Livemocha	Language—interact with native speakers
• Busuu	Practice a language skill
• My Happy Planet	Partner with a language member
Green- and civic-learning communities	
• Make Me Sustainable	Impact of the environment
• SocialVibe	Social causes—raise money
• Change.org	Participate for causes through petition
Scientific and academic-learning communities	
• ResearchGATE	Network for researchers and scientists
• Pronetos	Link scholars in a network
• Academia.edu	Community development to meet scholars
Education-related learning communities	
• TeacherTube	Community of educators share videos of instruction
• We The Teachers	Educators can meet, ask questions, share information
• TeachAde	Share lesson plans and different multimedia
Miscellaneous learning communities	
• LearnHub	Communities and lifelong learners
• GradeGuru	Community of college students
• Connexions	Rice University learning and study modules

Table 1. Communities that are free (LearningPath.org, 2016)

Another example of a virtual community is the language-learning community that was developed to help others with language interest. Individuals can join and share their skills, ask questions, and voice concerns. There is also a virtual community where participants who are interested in understanding the impact of the environment can help by raising money to support their cause and concerns.

Virtual communities not only have an academic focus but they may also provide users with a scientific focus. The focus of the scientific community is to establish a network with different researchers and scientists. The community provides those who are interested with a link to other scientist as well as other scholars. Linking with other scientists can be useful and important for conducting new and future research. The development of networks encourages participation, experimentation, and evaluation of concepts, which leads to new theories that will create a positive growth for our world.

The education network was developed for educators to come together to share resources, share their best practices, and also to ask questions that may be beneficial in developing lesson plans. As educators share ideas and resources, this opens the door for understanding how to improve teaching approaches, share new ideas, and compare best practices. The educator network can be beneficial for traditional classrooms, virtual classrooms, and virtual communities.

The benefit of the communities is that it brings individuals together. In each community, there needs to be etiquette and decorum. Everyone should feel that he or she is an active participant when discussing different topics and sharing information in the virtual community environment. Figures 2 and 3 provide a view of Livemocha and Teacherube, both of which are virtual communities.

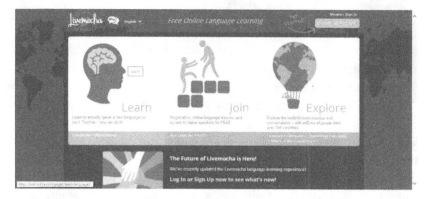

Figure 2. Livemocha Virtual Community (http://livemocha.com/)

Figure 3. TeacherTube (https://www.teachertube.com/)

APPROPRIATE BEHAVIOR

Individuals share information in a virtual community, forming a trust between all members' working toward a common goal. Members of a community want to make sure "that trust has as much of a key role to play in successful online learning as it has in face-to-face learning" (Anderson et al., 2011, p. 358). If there are rules and regulations for the face-to-face learning environment, there also need to be rules and regulations that build trust and thus relationships of the members are developed in the virtual learning environment. However, "it is much harder to establish in an online environment that is recognized by educators and is an ongoing focus of communications research trying to identify the components of trust" (Anderson et al., 2011, p. 358). Trust is important and teachers and students need to be able to abide by the guidelines and standards in order to build trust in the virtual community.

Members will want to establish trust and be recognized for their knowledge and contribution to the virtual community. As Chen et al. noted, "As community trust plays a fundamental role in enhancing knowledge sharing, exactly when the influence of community trust on individuals' knowledge sharing intentions would be augmented needs to be well understood" (Chen et al., 2014, p. 169). This is important because credibility encourages others to participate and this will increase the knowledge base of information. If there is trust, then "those with a high level of altruism are more likely to freely share information or discuss personal experiences in the community than those with a low level of altruism. We thus hypothesize that altruism is a moderator which augments" (Chen et al., 2014, p. 169). Promoting cohesiveness as well as trust forms a relationship that can be established between individuals of a community. As relationships are formed, virtual experiences will be shared and this will increase the usefulness of the virtual community.

When individuals understand the impact of their actions, the group will want to contribute and make a positive contribution to the group. According to Chen et al., "As people who trust each other, individuals who enjoy helping others are likely to exhibit greater knowledge sharing intention. For example, they would have a greater willingness to share information or discuss personal experiences in the community" (Chen et al., 2014, p. 170). The virtual community can be used to encourage trust as well as specific behavior where everyone can share information and their experience in the community.

Sharing information is the key to virtual community collaboration and critical to the growth of the virtual community. Effort is needed to make sure that the information is accurate, up to date, as well as beneficial to the group. The development of information that is used to increase the growth and understanding of knowledge will help the virtual community grow. E-collaboration and the development of a network of students and educators will be beneficial as they provide years of increased knowledge in the way of data, information, and knowledge. In Chapter 4, there will be a discussion of E-collaboration in an educational environment.

CHAPTER 4.
E-COLLABORATION IN AN
EDUCATIONAL ENVIRONMENT

E-Collaboration is important for virtual education as well as for a virtu-al community. Teachers, students, and staff can actively participate and provide critical feedback to manage and improve the virtual community environment. Al-Zoube (2009) noted that an e-collaborative environ-ment is also referred to as a virtual learning environment (VLE). A VLE is considered an "electronic platform that can be used to provide and track eLearning courses and enhance face-to-face instruction with online components" (Al-Zoube, 2009, p. 59). This is much like using a virtual learning community in that the VLE is an extension of the classroom providing hands-on experience working in a lab or an open forum en-vironment. The VLE can be considered an environment in which those who have something in common can participate and share information using virtual tools.

The VLE may be considered a "cloud computing based solution for build-ing a virtual and personal learning environment which combines a wide range of technology, and tools for education" (Al-Zoube, 2009, p. 59). Using VLE technology increases the options of additional methods to work with students outside the classroom. This extension of the course room can be used along with Web 2.0 technology that provides blogs, Wikis, and social networking as extensions to the virtual community en-vironment (Al-Zoube, 2009). The tools and environment are useful for managing and creating a social network useful for providing additional instructions on various topics. Teachers can use the tools for expanding and creating different options for e-learning.

Since technology has impacted teachers, cloud resources are tools where teachers can use them without a lot of familiarity. El-Seoud et al. noted that "cloud computing has many benefits in education (e.g., providing educational resource storage and databases, e-mails, educational appli-cations and tools for students and teachers and clients located all over the world involving in an educational program)" (El-Seoud et al., 2013, p.63). Since there are a lot of benefits to cloud computing, teachers who have an understanding of the benefits can use them to their advantage for creating a social network. The benefits provide alignment for storage, archiving, and programs. Also, alignment is needed to determine the best approach to store information in a database. Since there are many different forms of storage, the knowledge of the different types of storage is necessary so that teachers and staff can select the best approach as per their needs. Teachers and staff should take time to evaluate different techniques required to store information and select options that will be useful using cloud technology. Also, during the evaluation, teachers and staff need to discuss what security measures are needed and useful for storage.

El-Seoud et al. noted that cloud computing "provides a convenient, on-demand access to a centralized shared pool of computing resources that can be deployed by a minimal management overhead and with a great efficiency" (El-Seoud, 2013, p. 64). If there is a centralized shared pool of computing resources, the resources can be accessed and managed easily. An evaluation of the information can cut down on cost because of the centralized storage while increasing the effectiveness of resource usage. By having environments that are readily available, this will help encourage learning at any time.

El-Seoud et al. further discussed how "cloud environment resources are available to the students with no need of having deep knowledge about the cloud computing concepts" (El-Seoud et al., 2013, p. 64). Students need not have a technical knowledge of cloud computing, but they need to understand how a virtual community works and how to navigate through it. If an environment is easy to use, then the site can be efficiently managed, students can easily access the information, and teachers can monitor and check the progress of students. This increases the benefit for using the virtual community for schools and helps in minimizing cost while increasing learning options.

Benefits for schools include cost-effectiveness, no need for additional traditional servers, minimal maintenance, services that are provided by a professional service provider, not necessary for failures or upgrades and used a lot, archives are provided, and services are supported for educational benefits (El-Seoud et al., 2013). The benefits to schools can help in lowering the cost to students along with minimizing the cost to schools. Schools will not need as much in their budgets for IT equipment, software, and software upgrades. Also, teachers can concentrate more on teaching and less on technical requirements needed for the class.

TEACHERS

A teacher is an important resource for students when it comes to a virtual learning community. A teacher is pivotal in the development of lesson plans as well as teaching. These efforts are evaluated based on quality and planning on a day-to-day basis and can also be useful in the virtual cloud community.

Because technology is so critical in today's society, teachers need to understand the importance of cloud technology and how this can benefit them in the classroom as well as outside of it using virtual communities. Teachers need to understand that the cloud can handle a large amount of data and information that students can access and use at any time. The cloud can be used to share information with other students and staff through collaborative efforts outside of the classroom.

If teachers or students need to access additional information for a class, this can be done by creating specific cloud centers that would be in the virtual community. Teachers and staff can decide whether students should have access rights to set up additional areas within the cloud so that working groups on their own can be accomplished for handling their assigned tasks. Teachers can work with the cloud service providers to determine the type of service they want and how to access the service for creating the environment as well as to set up smaller groups within the cloud community.

Since teachers play a major role in the continual existence of a virtual community, mentoring and participating in the virtual community are needed. Teachers should have the ability to set up a virtual community to help virtual or traditional classroom topics and ideas develop further. This community can be useful for providing mentoring services associated with continual instructional development. This social network will be useful in helping individuals work together to share ideas as well as develop the community for new or existing classrooms.

Chard et al. noted that "social networks are used to reflect real world relationships that allow users to share information and form connections between one another, essentially creating dynamic Virtual Organizations" (Chard et al., 2010, p. 99). This is an important part of understanding how the virtual environment works as a community. Taking information and presenting it in a format that is easy to understand is useful for those who belong to the social network. There can be various formats, which may depend on the platform that the virtual community selects to use. The social networking can help build a relationship outside of the classroom and encourage a connection with others while building confidence and trust in the community.

Relationships built between those in the community encourage sharing and interacting that establishes positive relationships between students, teachers, and staff. Chard et al. "propose leveraging the pre-established trust formed through friend relationships within a social network to form a dynamic 'Social Cloud', enabling friends to share resources within the context of a social network" (Chard et al., 2010, p. 99). The concept of the "Social Cloud" can help to build learning relationships as well as social relationships that can be carried over into higher education and throughout a student's career.

The social network can be established through a social cloud and forms the basis for the virtual community using cloud technology. As relationships grow, individuals in the community will want to join together to form a social network and participate in a social cloud, which is another form of virtual community development. The social cloud will grow based on the topic of discussion and activities that are planned for the group and individuals.

Table 1 provides a representation of the various roles or relationships the virtual community may have and the activities associated with each group. The roles may change and develop as the community grows and changes. Changes may be managed by each group in a different way in order to achieve the goals and objectives for the virtual community.

Table 1. Roles and Responsibilities of Teachers, Students, and Staff
for a Virtual Environment

Teachers	Students	Staff
Team leader	Team participate	Team developer
Develop tasks	Participate in tasks	Develop tasks area
Intercede in problems	Discuss problem	Provide site for monitoring
Collaborate	Participate	Provide area assistance

The role that is critical for a virtual community is the teacher's role. Teachers are considered the team leaders and are necessary for developing tasks for students. Teachers are also important for helping to manage and solve problems that may occur in a community. As team leaders, teachers are necessary for collaborating and facilitating discussions.

Based on the relationships and roles for students noted in Table 1, the role of the student is to participate in their team groups and participate in active tasks. Students can discuss different problems that arise and participate in active ongoing discussions. A student's role is to be an active participant and to encourage others to participate. Students may do this by asking questions, providing additional research about topics to discuss, and critically evaluating topics of discussion.

The staff members, as noted in Table 1, are responsible for managing administrative tasks such as setting up the teams and the task areas. They are also responsible for monitoring the virtual community site and providing technical support when needed. They should be trained on the platform and understand how the information is stored and archived.

Letitia noted many different roles and responsibilities for teachers that include providing guidelines, developing different tasks, and determining team development assignments. This creates a position of responsibility where teachers need to be available to intercede and monitor the virtual community while assisting students as well as interacting and collaborating through active discussions (Letitia, 2012, p. 203). Teachers can be quite interactive in the virtual community as well as they can participate and encourage other students to participate. The goal is to work toward accomplishing tasks based on a schedule developed for additional learning opportunities.

Diaz discussed "numerous teaching and learning opportunities and challenges that institutions face in adopting and implementing cloud-based technologies into their e-learning programs and provides a guide for forming implementation decisions" (Diaz, 2011, p. 95). Because of several challenges, there may be some resistance to implementing changes. Changes need to be discussed with all those involved and then shared with students. Changes will impact the successful implementation of the cloud computing environment. These changes are based on what colleges and universities want and whether or not they see the virtual community as a necessary part of the learning environment. So changes need to be addressed to make sure that the school agrees with the changes and that they feel that the virtual community is an important part of the virtual, traditional or face-to-face classroom.

Diaz (2011) suggested that "the emergence and proliferation of cloud-based tools has widened the gap between faculty member and student use of technology and has also presented some support and faculty development difficulties" (Diaz, 2011, p. 95). Since changes are not readily accepted by everyone, communication is the key to providing information on a regular basis and early in the process of planning change. Not all teachers and instructors can keep up with new technology or even want the new changes. Teachers may find it difficult to manage a virtual community because of the lack of equipment, knowledge of the virtual community, and its function.

In order to facilitate this, management should help support the effort by providing grants and budget allocations to assist instructors in obtaining the necessary technology, training, and support for the virtual community. Training and additional support should also be made available to staff to help plan, design, and develop the platform. By working through the changes that are planned, staff and teachers can work together to evaluate various platforms while planning a move to a new learning approach beneficial for the students.

As noted in Chapter 3, various platforms and tools can be downloaded and evaluated using demos that are free and available to the teacher to review and test. Providing information and data on various tools and platforms is necessary. As Diaz discussed, "Faculty members correctly assert that while today's students do in fact enter our institutions having had some exposure to Web 2.0 tools such as Facebook™, they lack an awareness of how those tools can be used for learning" (Diaz , 2011, p. 97). Even though our society has moved more and more to Web 2.0 and the Internet, there are still teachers, staff, and students who do not have technical expertise to work with many different types of technologies, tools, and platforms. Students may understand how to use the basic forms of social media such as Facebook, Twitter, and MySpace, but they may lack an understanding of other types of social media tools as it is related to virtual education.

That is why a teacher is instrumental in the virtual environment for guiding students in a direction to increase their social media knowledge. The teacher can act as a focal point and share their knowledge to help students develop skills for using tools to assist in their learning and knowledge development. Teachers need to understand the role they play in the virtual learning community and its impact and effect on students and their progress. Not only do teachers play a major role in the virtual community but also students have a role that impacts the success or failure of the virtual community.

STUDENTS

So what is the student's role in the virtual community? Students are responsible for taking tasks that are assigned and turning it into useful information that can be used to increase knowledge and move toward career growth. This is achieved through additional assignments, questions, additional research, and sharing information topics related to assignments. These activities can occur through an ongoing collaboration in the virtual community environment between teachers and students or students and students.

Chard et al. discussed how "social networking has become an everyday part of many peoples' lives as evidenced by the huge user communities" (Chard et al., 2010, p. 99). As individuals become more familiar with different types of technologies, there is an increase in social interaction and community development growth. This can be valuable as students are exposed to new and improved methods of communication and social media tools. As the social community increases, there is a development of ideas and information that can be used to increase knowledge and expand the network. Since our society has moved more and more toward social media and social connectivity, understanding various types of social media is necessary.

As a part of collaborative learning, Beer, Slack, and Armitt noted that it is "important when developing distributed collaborative learning environments to design an appropriate structure in which students can meet online and learn together in a wide variety of different groupings that form naturally to support each stage of the learning process" (Beer, Slack, & Armitt, 2005, p. 30). Determining the correct environment that meets the most students' learning styles and impacts the learning process is essential. It is important to not only introduce various techniques of social networking but also to provide students with a structure on how to achieve their community and educational goals through collaboration based on a diversified group of individuals. This can be achieved by scheduling specific times and groups of individuals who share the same interest and learning style.

The comfort level of using various tools is noted when Diaz discussed that "on the other hand, faculty members may have noticed that entering students have a heightened comfort level in existing in the type of digital environment that has the potential to be connected with learning" (Diaz, 2011, p. 97). Some students have an interest in communicating through social networking and may thrive in such type of environment. However, there are some students who face difficulty in communicating and collaborating with other students in a social networking environment. Teachers need to determine which students would benefit from social networking in the cloud environment and also how to pair up different learning styles with different individuals. Students who not only have the same interest but also those who share the same approach to learning should be paired together. Diaz discussed how students "deal with a trial-and-error approach to tool use and change in general and often have had a broad exposure to a variety of different web based software and hardware tools" (Diaz, 2011, p. 97). Trial and error is a strategic approach when evaluating different tools and platforms because certain platforms and tools may or may not be usable and workable in all situations. As students become familiar with different types of technologies, they will also benefit by testing different technologies to see which one provides the best approach to their individual learning style. Staff may also find that testing can assist students in selecting tools based on the type of technology they have and want to use for the virtual community.

STAFF

So what is the role of a staff member in a virtual community? Staff members may be involved in scheduling, training, administrative tasks, and evaluating the virtual community. They may assist student learning by being available to schedule, train, and evaluate the virtual community environment. This should be done in collaboration with the teacher and management. Scheduling of events is important and as students and teachers become a part of the virtual community, adequate space and room for different virtual community tasks and functions need to be assessed and scheduled.

The scheduling process may include mapping different days of a week for webinar events and training in addition to virtual meetings for the community. These events are important for the virtual community as this will help to understand how to create, view, assess, evaluate, and archive information. Staff can be instrumental in helping students and teachers work through different administrative areas in the community and share information in a way that is constructive for all participants. Training can occur through training seminars and discussion forums set up in the community. Staff members can also help to manage the information and archive the information for student and teacher use. Also, staff members can manage database requests and post the information for the virtual community to use on a regular basis.

Facilitating communication and sharing information is what Beer et al. suggested. They noted that "social networks provide a platform to facilitate communication and sharing between users, therefore modeling real world relationships" (Beer et al., 2005, p. 99). As communication increases so does staffing needs to facilitate manage and store the data. The staff may play a pivotal role in keeping up with the information in order to help the virtual community be effective and useful.

Information can be shared that provide users with real-world simulations and real-world experience. As noted by El-Seoud et al., "Web-based evaluation has the advantage of instant feedback, and appropriate questions could be added, and ease of statistical analysis" (El-Seoud et al., 2013, p. 66). As individuals become familiar with the environment, they will enjoy the interaction, feedback, and the ability to ask questions that will facilitate the learning process. Everyone wants immediate responses to his or her questions and concerns, and the virtual environment can be useful for its 24/7 availability, which can be used to increase access and interaction between teachers, students, and staff. As more and more individuals access the system, statistics on the usage will be valuable for determining the time of a day when there is most activities. Monitoring and recording activities can be useful to help determine if more services are needed and at what is the peak time when service should be increased.

Statistical evaluation can be useful in assisting staff with the evaluation and collection of information. This information, in turn, can be used to determine the effectiveness of the virtual community. A useful tool may be a questionnaire that can be developed and provided to students, teachers, and staff to gather information on the effectiveness of the community: How individuals use the community, is there enough interest in the topics, and is there enough communication and interaction to keep the virtual community active?

Table 2. Goals of the Virtual Community

Overall goals of the virtual community
Increase awareness of the topic
Create collaboration
Establish a cohesive group
Determine an effective way to communicate
Gather and maintain current and archival information

In Table 2, there are various goals a virtual community may want to achieve and work toward. Establishing goals may be useful for teachers, students, and staff. Keeping a set of goals can be useful as this can help the community know if they are meeting the objectives established for it. For example, a goal may include how to increase the awareness of different topics discussed in the classroom. Another goal may be how to create a collaborative and cohesive group of students who share the same interests. The goal of increased communication may also be useful in finding ways to open channels of learning in order to determine whether students are reaching their academic goals.

The virtual community environment approach to communication and interaction will help the community to grow and excel with the concept of increase communication and interaction with students who share common interests. Gathering and maintaining current and archival information can be valuable to see what has been accomplished as well as what are the possible areas for the future growth of the community.

Table 3. Goals of the Teachers, Students, and Staff

Goals for teachers	Goals for students	Goals for staff
Provide guidance	Determine the amount of information to be used for each session	Develop scheduling
Enter names of individuals interested in the community	Form groups of similar interest and determine a method of communication	Provide support and training for those who request it
Help the group focus on specific topics	Work with those who have similar interests and goals to increase group awareness	Maintain the database of information and work toward maintaining files in chronological order

Table 3 breaks down the goals of teachers, students, and staff. The goals for teachers are to provide guidance and information to different individuals who are interested in the virtual community that may work together. Also, teachers are responsible for helping groups focus on specific topics.

The goals for students in the virtual community may be to determine the amount of information that will be used for specific sessions. Various groups may form based on specific information and this is important for those with similar interest as well as for keeping up using different modes of communication. Students may also work with those who have a similar interest as well as the same goals. This type of group dynamic can increase the group awareness and increase knowledge and skills.

The goals for the staff may include scheduling as well as providing support and training for anyone in the virtual community who may need it. The staff may also manage the database and the information so the files are kept in a controllable manner. In Chapter 5, there will be a discussion on the development of virtual communities and the importance of technology and collaboration.

CHAPTER 5.
DEVELOPMENT OF VIRTUAL COMMUNITIES

DEVELOPING THE COMMUNITY—
UNDERSTANDING THE TECHNOLOGY

In Chapter 3, there was a discussion on the challenges that virtual communities face when using cloud technology. As technology continues to develop, analyzing how to keep the virtual community up to date is essential. Options for verifying and validating technology are needed to ensure that it is up to date and is vital to its success. Schools often lack resources for keeping technology up to date; however, utilizing free technology can make it easier on the budget.

Cloud technology continues to grow and Lee noted that "this term of 'Cloud' first emerged in the 1990s, and usually an icon of 'Cloud' has been symbolizing the entire Internet networks since and until today" (Lee, 2012, p. 5712). The term "Cloud" continues to be a buzz word, although colleges and universities have turned cloud computing into a reality. Because of this, it is further noted that after conducting research, it was determined that "procurement and installation of cloud computing technologies investment such as internet teaching, internet databases, network software and hardware equipment for the case school's implementation of innovative change indeed has an absolutely positive effect on inner-and-outer orientated organizational effectiveness" (Lee, 2012, p. 5718). This positive approach to virtual education has opened up the usage of networking in many different areas. Procuring the services and understanding that the installation of various types of cloud technologies can involve different tools and equipment. The evaluation of tools can be part of a process for setting up the cloud service that is based on the provider's services. Different types of services can encourage the interaction and socialization between groups, students, staff, and students.

The interaction between individuals is what Baglieri and Consoli suggested because "virtual communities allow people who interact to satisfy their own needs and to share purpose such as an interest, need, information exchange, or service that provides a reason for the community" (Baglieri & Consoli, 2009, p. 354). The virtual community can be a key to a positive approach to understanding new topics, exchanging information, and increase data awareness. This increased knowledge in different topic areas can foster an interest in pursuing advanced research for a specific topic. This additional research can be performed in a virtual community if the community has been set up and aligned with the required research tools.

The alignment of resources with cloud technology can be managed by a service provider, school, and staff. This alignment of resources is necessary in order to provide a consistent method of information exchange for research. There cannot be an exchange of information and ideas, but as the community grows, so the development of trust between individuals in the community. Trust will form a cohesive bond between the individuals in the community and provide a sense of purpose and drive. The cohesive trust and bond can occur locally or on a global basis depending on who is using the community.

Trust in a virtual community is essential and Anderson et al. suggested that "trust between the partners, among the students, between the educators, in the laboratories, in the technology and across international borders are all key issues to be negotiated if this partnership is to succeed" (Anderson et al., 2011, p. 357). As the community develops so the partnership between those who participate, which can even encourage new partnership development. A collaborative cohesive trust that is built between all participants in the community can foster an increased interaction. Trust is developed that will encourage participation and form partnerships between individuals, which, in turn, will foster a harmonious collaboration of ideas and data.

Anderson et al. further discussed how "trust is a multidimensional word, although its meanings all seem to be based on relationships, bonds, confidence and vulnerabilities of one kind or another" (Anderson et al., 2011, p. 357). Trust can be built on relationships and can be used to build confidence in the community. As confidence continues to grow, community participants will engage in an active way that will steer the community in a positive direction.

COLLABORATING TO KEEP THE COMMUNITY GOING

Getting the community up and running can be a challenge. Therefore, collaboration and cooperation are essential. Baglieri and Consoli (2009) noted earlier that there are key areas that are important to be considered when a community is set up and developed. As individuals participate in a community, they also consider how the community can be beneficial for their own purpose. Participants need to let those in the community who have the same interest and feel free to exchange information that will enrich the community. Some members may feel shy about sharing ideas. In such cases, trust can be an important part of the process in order to encourage their active and open participation.

The community should develop guidelines to help establish how information will be shared and how participation will impact the community. There is also technology that can be implemented to track the social connection and provide information on the amount of activity for the entire group (Baglieri & Consoli, 2009). This can be useful to determine if additional room is needed and whether different interaction and participation may be useful.

Baglieri and Consoli noted that "on the other hand, the successful operation of a virtual community depends largely on whether these organizations have a comprehensive understanding of the essence of a virtual community" (Baglieri & Consoli, 2009, p. 356). This is critical, and management needs to understand the focus, needs, and the future goals and direction of the community. The essence of the community is built not only on trust but also on the understanding of the goals and objectives necessary to keep the community focused and organized.

Keng, Hui-Ying, and Ya-Ting (2011) provided information, as illustrated in Table 1, that shows four different features that are considered useful and needed as a part of the virtual community:

Table 1. Features Shared in an Online/Virtual Community

Features shared in the online virtual community
The need to belong and identify with the community
Making an impact by influencing the group to understand the individual value
Being supported by others in the community
Sharing experience and comradery

The features that are noted in Table 1 are the areas that can positively or negatively impact the virtual community. For example, the virtual community provides users with an identity that increases the need to belong. This, in turn, creates cohesiveness and adds value to the community through the exchange of ideas and information. As individuals are supported by the community, this brings about support not only with each other in the community but also with those who support the community. This is useful and increases comradery that can be shared not only with the current virtual community but also with other virtual communities through virtual interaction. This comradery can be channeled into the virtual community in the form of a learning community.

Heath et al. noted that "learning communities gained attention in 1984 after the publication of the "involvement in Learning" report, which was sponsored by the U.D. Education Department" (Heath et al., 2005, p. 33). The learning community is useful for getting individuals involved and this is supported by those in educational positions. The learning community provides commitment in learning and improves and promotes learning. This form of learning provides individuals in the community with knowledge associated with different educational programs.

The educational systems efficacy relies on policies and practices based on policies related to student involvement and increased learning (Heath et al., 2005, p. 33). Policies are an important part of the total process of student involvement, evaluating technology, and technology changes for the virtual community. Since technology continually changes, monitoring the community and keeping the technology up to date are critical. Policies for the school technology changes need to be managed and evaluated particularly as they impact curriculum that is an area that needs continual assessment.

INCORPORATING VIRTUAL COMMUNITIES INTO THE CURRICULUM

As teachers develop curriculum, different areas need to be considered for the virtual community that will impact the delivery and incorporation of the curriculum. Different guidelines and standards for the virtual classroom and the virtual community may affect how curriculum is developed and used in the virtual community. Since the virtual community is considered an extension of the virtual classroom or the face-to-face traditional classroom, the development of additional materials and resources may be necessary. Teachers may think that this is just additional work that needs to be developed, but actually providing additional resources and materials may enhance the virtual classroom and make the delivery of the traditional curriculum more attractive.

Chang discussed how a "collaborative learning theory and practice can be applied and used to support the creation of an online learning community" (Chang, 2012, p. 154). The collaborative learning theory was developed and notes how students can engage in activities to encourage a collaborating sharing approach to learning. Chang further noted that "individual learners connect and learn how to use VLE technology to support one another and create a genuine and collaborative learning community" (Chang, 2012, p. 154). This form of support increases a collaborative sharing approach to learning and mimics a real-world environment for problem solving and collaborative behavior. The virtual learning environment can be used to interact, connect, and cooperate in a learning process where students can work with each other and exchange information and ideas for future research. This collaborative and interactive approach to learning opens up a discussion format for sharing and interacting with other students.

Armstrong and Thornton noted that "one strategy is to move away from lecture and toward conversation as a way of teaching" (Armstrong & Thornton, 2012, p. 1). The teachers approach to include discussion as part of the interaction of learning is a great way to get feedback and determine the level of knowledge. The key to the discussion approach for the teacher is to be interactive and help guide the discussions and provide critical questioning that will further the discussions.

An effective approach to increase the communication for virtual learning is to set up discussion boards, manage the boards and participate in the discussions. The instructor needs to encourage students to participate and elicit answers from students by providing critical questions. This critical questioning process can be used to encourage students to not only provide an answer but to think about many possible approaches for answering the question. This approach changes a simple answer to a question to a complex structured answer which can be used as a critical review and analysis of different solutions to the answer.

Helping students think further than a yes or no answer can be useful and increase participation for virtual activities and virtual discussions. This increased activity can be used to engage students in more than one activity and increase the student's ability to further analyze complex information. Armstrong and Thornton (2012) suggested that it would be beneficial to blend an online active "discussion with online asynchronous discussion" (p. 2). Therefore you can combine and blend the learning activities by meeting virtually in a real-time manner and then follow-up with additional discussions in an asynchronous discussion.

"An instructional strategy may be implemented that leverages the structure, time for deep reflection, and critical thinking associated with asynchronous online learning, and the social and emotional characteristics of face-to-face communications in fast-paced, oral discourse" (Armstrong & Thornton, 2012, p. 2). The combination of synchronous and asynchronous discussions can be beneficial to the teacher and the students through a Socrates method of questioning and answering. With the combination of the two discussion techniques the student is not only answering questions but thinking beyond a yes/no response and looking for additional ways to analyze and answer questions to achieve a further in-depth response for the a question.

Encouraging virtual discussions by actively participating in a synchronous discussion that is set up virtually for students can be beneficial and reflects the commitment not only from the student but also from the teacher. As students become comfortable in the discussion forum, this can also increase their comfort when working in groups in an asynchronous fashion, which is a part of the virtual community. The asynchronous discussions can be just as productive as face-to-face synchronous discussions if teachers and students are motivated to interact and exchange information. Asynchronous discussions allow the students to develop their responses to posted questions ahead of time, thereby allowing time to reflect and research their answers. This type of discussion format also allows the students to engage in analysis and feedback to other students' responses.

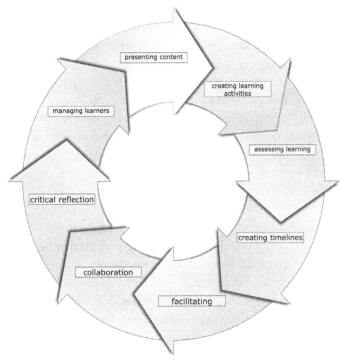

Figure 1. Teacher's Responsibility in the Virtual Community.

Figure 1 provides an illustration of the importance a teacher's role plays in the virtual community. Teachers need to be able to develop content, present the content, create learning activities, assess learning, create timelines, facilitate, collaborate, critically reflect, and manage students. The content development may be lessons, information, and discussions. Development of learning activities can be used to help expand the learning community by creating areas of research that will expand the topics that may be discussed in class. The teacher can assess learning and create timelines for facilitating and collaborating with students. This facilitating and collaboration will provide a critical reflection and management of the students.

The responsibility of the teacher can take on many different forms which Armstrong and Thornton (2012) suggested as "those responsibilities that traditionally belong to the teacher including: presenting content, creating learning activities, assessing learning, creating timelines, facilitating purposeful collaboration and critical reflection, and scaffolding learners" (p. 2). The teacher's role is critical in the virtual community as an extension of the classroom and the responsibilities noted above are all considered a way to manage and interact with the students.

As students work in their virtual community, they may also take on some of the activities that teachers generally engage in for managing the virtual environment. For example, students can provide their review of the content in the classroom and become active in self-centered learning. This is useful in determining whether they are learning information, understanding the content, and can actively work on their own which is necessary for the virtual community.

The different learning styles of students may change the form of collaborative learning and critical reflection because of the diverse approaches to learning. As noted in Figure 1 the development of learning activities is critical because teachers need to be able to assess learning and create information based on different learning styles. Teachers manage different learning activities by developing lesson plans that include timelines for managing information, noting needed changes in curriculum, applying different lesson plans to different learning styles. Each of the aforementioned are all areas that need to be evaluated in order to facilitate effective collaborative learning using distance learning techniques.

Distance learning settings are an area Campbell and Ellingson (2010) noted that "online classes and other distance learning settings, however, can make it challenging to introduce traditional group projects" (p. 83). When teachers make use of the virtual learning community, they can adapt their traditional projects into a format that students can use to not only focus their attention in a group but as an individual learner and achieve the same results as a traditional setting. Different techniques and technology are needed depending on the learning situation and approach to the learning process.

Different technology is what Campbell and Ellingson (2010) noted when they discussed how "Wikis use technology to facilitate group work in distance learning settings" (p. 83). Wikis are useful when working in the virtual collaborative environment because of the group dynamics that can be developed. Campbell and Ellingson (2010) suggested that "Wikis allow individuals in different locations to asynchronously post and edit content on a website to iteratively and cooperatively work toward a solution" (p. 83). It is noted in the virtual community that a collaborative effort of the Wiki is the ability to share information with students on an asynchronous basis.

Campbell and Ellingson (2010) further noted that "student feedback on their experiences using wikis as well as instructor observations were mostly positive while negative comments were primarily administrative in nature and easily addressed" (p. 83). As noted from the results of the research by Campbell and Ellingson (2010), the Wiki can be a useful tool for sharing information and is considered part of virtual learning when specifically directed through lessons and assignments. There may be administrative issues such as downtime and difficulty logging on when the network is down making it difficult to have the network 24/7. Working through networking issues can produce a positive approach for students and teachers so schools will have a constructive experience using Wikis. Not only Wikis but also networking with other schools can bring about a positive virtual experience.

NETWORKING WITH OTHER SCHOOLS

As students build their virtual network they are also building a strong network by collaborating with others. This network can grow and become efficient and successful as students participate and share information. Forming a network alliance with other schools in the district can be beneficial; this can grow regionally as well as grow on a state level with goals to go to an international level. Chang (2012) noted that "those who did not study in pairs and groups actually collaborated with others both inside and outside the class" (p. 157). Setting up collaborative groups not only in the virtual classroom but also as a virtual community would be beneficial to students who may have difficulty working in paired groups but may want to have the ability to exchange ideas outside the classroom more on an individual person to person approach.

Collaboration and feedback have been advantageous as Chang (2012) further noted by discussing that "collaboration, feedback, which refers to exchanges between students and students, and between students and the teacher. Receiving feedback from the teacher and from their peers created for some students a sense of community of learning together" (p. 158). The feedback can be used to stimulate and create a diversified approach to new learning as well as giving the students a feeling of belonging to the group. The feedback received should encourage critical thinking and be used to collaborate outside their immediate area increasing communication with other schools. This community of learning demonstrates the usefulness of collaboration and feedback that can be achieved in courses and topics that may need additional explanations. Teachers and students can work together to decide which topics they want to expand on and which topics would be beneficial for the student to work on by addressing additional discussions and collaborative research.

The virtual community can network with other schools that may be working on the same topics engage in virtual conversations and discussions. Also students can compare and contrast their findings and determine whether future research would be beneficial. As the virtual communities continue to grow continual evaluation of the community is necessary and the development and monitoring of the community will increase the demands so careful planning is necessary.

PLANNING FOR THE VIRTUAL COMMUNITY

Planning the goals, objectives, and purpose will impact the steps needed for setting up and managing the cloud service and the virtual community. Following is a systematic approach of steps for working through the planning, analysis, and setup of the virtual community. These steps are also presented in Table 2:

1. **Cloud Provider**—Look for a cloud provider that meets the specific needs of the cloud community. As the idea of virtual communities begins to take shape, evaluating cloud providers is an important first step. Software Insider (2016) provided a comparison between different cloud providers, services, and cost (Software Insider, 2016). The Software Insider evaluated and compared services based on different models which may be an IaaS (Infrastructure as a Service), the base rate for pricing (based on the usage per hour), the deployment model which may be a hybrid cloud, or a public cloud. Also the providers can be evaluated on different server operating systems. Some are Windows or Linux servers.

2. **Tools**—Select the tools for building the virtual platform—ZDnet presented a listing of 10 possible tools to use for setting up a virtual community that includes, Zoomla, Drupal, PHP-Nuke, Zikula, SharePoint community portal, Lithium, Dotnetnuke, community server, KickApps, and Jive. Each of the aforementioned offer specific content management features. There are several examples of the abovementioned tools in Chapters 2 and 3.

3. **Platform**—Set up the platform—Setting up the platform involves selecting and assessing different platforms before determining which platform best meets the needs of the community. It is important to select the best platform that meets the needs of the community and then develop the platform based on the requirements of the community.

4. **Load content**—The content can be developed and loaded using a template format so there is consistency from topic to topic. Each platform will have specific instructions on how to load and post the information for the community. The content platform will be used to manage the students, teacher, and staff support and for keeping track of the information, scheduling and evaluation.

5. **Load students**—Students can be loaded into the system. Administrative rights need to be given to the staff and teachers for keeping and managing the system up to date with the content.

6. **Security/Admin**—Administrators are important for managing the content, platform, and students. Administrators can be staff or teachers. The security of the data is also important and the administrator is key for making sure that the information, data, and

student information is secured.

7. **Accessibility**—Accessibility needs to be addressed and there should also be testing on the platform to make sure that 508 accessibility standards are followed. There are specific 508 standards and guidelines that are necessary to follow so everyone can access the community as well as be a part of the community. Section508.gov is the GSA Government-wide website that provides information on the law of accessibility as well as applicable parts of the 508 standards—http://www.section508.gov/.

8. **Global**—After the virtual community is developed, the management of the community becomes critical. This means that in order to globalize the virtual community, it would be necessary to determine connections and security so that other communities can access and combine with the community. Globalization may involve working in the community on a district, region, or international level. The development of the virtual community and the steps noted before are important for moving toward the setup of the cloud computing service and the cloud community.

Table 2. Steps for Setting up the Virtual Community

Task	Responsible Party
Look for Cloud Provider	Management/Teacher
Select Tools for building Online Community	Management/Teacher
Develop the Platform	Staff/Teacher
Load Content	Staff/Teacher
Load Students	Staff/Teacher
Security/Admin	Staff
Accessibility	Staff
Global/Networking	Teacher/Students

Each of the steps noted in Table 2 can be assigned a party to be responsible for the planning, analysis and evaluation of each step. Communication between all parties is necessary before moving from step to step.

Now that the steps have been identified for setting up the virtual community, it is necessary to look at the development of the cloud technology and its impact on the virtual classroom. In Chapter 6, there will be a discussion about the development of cloud technology that addresses servers, security, classroom setup, resources, and archives.

CHAPTER 6.
DEVELOPMENT OF CLOUD TECHNOLOGY

VIRTUAL COMMUNITY—SERVERS, SECURITY

Cloud technology can be positive for a virtual community because it can assist in many different services. Cloud computing architecture needs to be understood by teachers and staff members in order to create an efficient system. Software as a service (SaaS), platform as a service (PaaS), and infrastructure as a service (IaaS) can be used to set up a SaaS software package, a PaaS platform, and an IaaS infrastructure. SaaS is a service and is used as the cloud server accessed through an Internet connection. This software is used by those who want to pay for the resource and have access to the cloud service. By using this service, the school only pays for what they want on the cloud and this minimizes storage and space on the school server secured with an SSL protocol.

PaaS is defined as a platform as a service. This feature can offer the school a platform that can be used to create an application so installing an application is not necessary. Web interfaces and applications are part of a PaaS model. IaaS is an infrastructure service that is a virtual provider, storage site and a virtualized hardware source. IaaS is considered part of the disk space and memory for the servers (Mitakos, Almaliotis, Diakakis, & Demerouti, 2014, p. 23). Figure 1 provides an important representation of the cloud architecture for the cloud computing environment and demonstrates that users can utilize different parts of the architecture when accessing cloud services. This type of storage is important to understand and individual users can access each part of the architecture when needed.

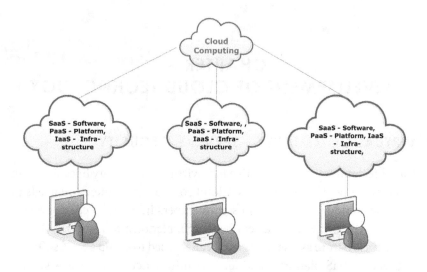

Figure 1. Cloud Computing Architecture.

Storage services may vary and Alzain, Soh, and Pardede noted that "there are many features of cloud computing. Firstly, cloud storage services such as Amazon S3 or Microsoft SkyDrive (Now One Drive) allow consumers to access their data online" (Alzain, Soh, & Pardede, 2012, p. 51). When evaluating the different cloud service options, look at the different services in order to compare and evaluate the service that best meets the needs of the cloud community and become familiar with the different terminology.

It is important to understand some of the basic terminology in order to recognize which cloud service provider meets the needs of the community. For example, a public cloud is considered an area that many different individuals can access for the service and work collaboratively along with other individuals. There are advantages and disadvantages for public cloud service. An example of a disadvantage is performance issues that may slow down usage causing bottlenecks on the cloud. Advantages of the public cloud are that users have the ability to access the service when needed. The private cloud environment has its own virtual location that limits access from public groups. The private cloud environment provides users with the ability to have more control over their environment while increasing the flexibility and management of the system (Angeles, 2014).

Both public and private services provide specific features, so understanding what each offers and how to obtain the service is needed. Evaluating different services is important to make sure that the right environment is used to support the virtual community.

Amazon S3 is a simple storage service that can be used to store information and keep it secure. The service provides an interface that can be used to store and manage data. This storage service does not include a fee associated with the service so no setup costs are required (Amazon Web Services, 2016). Another cloud service is SkyDrive which is now called OneDrive. This cloud service can be used to store information and images. It is noted that photos and documents can be stored free up to 15 gigabytes (Microsoft, 2016).

Understanding how different cloud services can be used is shown in Figure 2 which suggests that large populations can access the cloud service using different technology. For example individuals can use the computer, tablet or a mobile device to interact with a cloud service. Figure 2 is a representation of how users that use different platforms can interact at the same time using cloud technology.

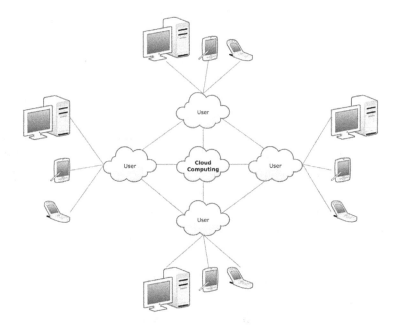

Figure 2. Cloud Users and the Cloud.

Alzain et al. discussed how "cloud services have been built over the internet, any issue that is related to internet security will also affect cloud services" (Alzain et al., 2012, p. 55). A cloud service will not only offer the cloud as a service but also provide security to ensure information and data is secured. Security is based on the infrastructure the cloud service provides and network functions. Alzain et al. noted how "resources in the cloud are accessed through the internet; consequently, even if the cloud provider focuses on security in the cloud infrastructure, the data is still transmitted to the users through the network, which may be insecure" (Alzain et al., 2012, p. 55). This is a concern so the network also needs to have security as the information is transmitted. That is why it is necessary when looking for a cloud service provider to understand the functions of the cloud infrastructure, networking services and how the information is secured. Figure 3 illustrates different cloud computing technologies that are used for cloud computing using different cloud infrastructure.

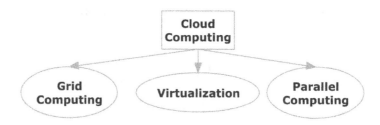

Figure 3. Cloud Computing Makes Use of Different Technologies

Cloud technology can be based on three different technologies about which Militaru et al. discussed when defining how "cloud computing technology is the result of convergence of three main directions of technological development such as grid computing, virtualization, and parallel computing" (Militaru et al. 2013, p. 213). Each of these technologies provides the basic parts of cloud computing technology. Cano-Lopez (2005) noted that grid computing is based on a network of computers and through the grouping of computers, clusters are managed with different servers (see Figure 4).

Martinez discussed how "grid computing requires that physical computing resources are made available as a shared pool of computing power, with the workload distributed across this in a dynamic manner" (Martinez, 2005, p. 12). Distributing the workload is necessary in order for the grid to accommodate a large number of users. It is important to develop "a grid which is a set of independent computers that are combined into a unified system through system software and standard networking technologies" (Martinez, 2005, p. 12). Figure 4 provides a representation of how grid computing can be set up and how there is an interaction between all users that flow into a control node.

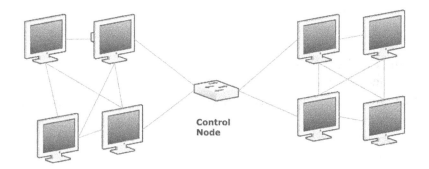

Figure 4. Grid Computing

The unification of the systems or virtualization is another aspect of cloud. Virtualization can be managed through a set of independent computers. Johnston noted that "virtual machine technologies enable one physical workstation or server to run multiple operating systems and related applications at the same time" (Johnston, 2008, p. 19). This provides a cost savings for the school since multiple systems can run in tandem increasing performance. Along with grid technology Johnston noted that "a virtual machine uses virtualization software and selected hardware devices to create an emulated operating environment" (Johnston, 2008, p. 19). The emulation of the environment can be managed easily by understanding how a virtualized computer environment works and how the virtualization can assist in working in a cloud environment.

By emulating or mirroring an environment, the school can reduce costs and server time allowing more students to work in the community environment. In this way cloud computing achieves the following, reduction in cost savings in servers and efficiency with storage. Along with grid computing and virtualization another important area of cloud computing is parallel computing.

Joshi and Ram (1999) discussed how "parallel computing on tightly coupled distributed systems has so far been widely popular. However, recent advances in communication technology and processor technology make parallel programming on loosely coupled distributed systems, especially on interconnected workstations, a viable and attractive proposition" (p.76). Joshi and Ram (1999) further noted that "there are several key issues that distinguish parallel computing on workstation clusters from that of tightly coupled massively parallel architectures" (p.76). In Figure 5, it is clear to see how SAAS, IAAS, and PAAS along with grid, virtual, and parallel computing all work in tandem to make a successful and useful cloud environment. Key elements of a successful cloud environment include the software, framework, hosting, database synchronization, grid computing, virtualization, parallel computing, and platform visualization. Figure 5 provides a representation of the architecture and technology.

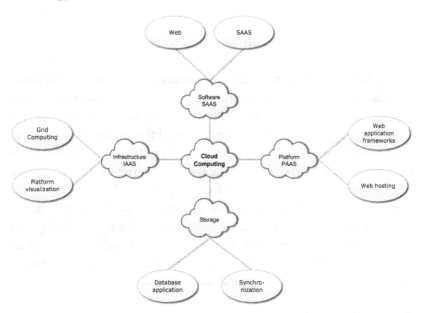

Figure 5. Cloud Technology

Since there are many aspects of cloud computing that can be managed as Militaru et al. suggested "cloud computing delivers a variety of software and hardware services such as virtual servers, storage, applications, and processing power over the internet" (Militaru, 2013, p. 214). Servers are necessary for a virtual environment that can handle storage, applications, and process information over the Internet. Software is needed to make the virtual environment successful and useful to teachers and students. Understanding how the servers and software impact the setup for the virtual community, it is necessary to understand how this will impact the classroom with access, setup, resources, and archives.

CLASSROOM— ACCESS, SETUP, RESOURCES, ARCHIVES

For a successful community of practice, Campbell and Uys noted that "there are identifiable features to a successful community of practice, and most importantly the ability to sustain the community" (Campbell & Uys, 2007, p. 19). Managing the virtual community needs to have someone in place that has features of leadership, participation, distinguishable boundaries and the ability to be a part of the environment. Someone that manages the virtual community and leads the virtual community provides guidance and structure through communication and active participation.

Managing the environment and keeping the information up to date will keep the environment reliable. The environment will thrive and exist on accurate up to date information and resources. Militaru, Niculescu, and Teaha 2013 further suggested that "cloud user's access these services through the cloud. End users do not know often anything about the location where their data are processed" (Militaru, Niculescu, & Teaha 2013, p. 214). That is why it is important for teachers and staff to have a good understanding of the architecture, security, and setup of the virtual community environment. As teachers and staff become familiar with the virtual community environment, they can share their knowledge with students and then this becomes a collaborative effort for maintaining an efficient and useful virtual community.

STUDENT COLLABORATION— ACCESS, RESOURCES, ARCHIVES

As trust is developed in the virtual community, Campbell and Uys noted that "communication builds trust. Communication along with trust is a fundamental to building communities, allowing them to grow, change, and achieve objectives" (Campbell & Uys, 2007, p.21). This is an important factor when developing the virtual community and a continued effort is needed as the community grows. Dasgupta, Granger, and McGarry (2002) discussed how student collaboration is useful in virtual communities and there are areas where e-collaboration provides for specific categories such as email and chats. Groups can support virtual members and provide suites of software that encourage collaboration and communication. For the virtual community there can be synchronous and asynchronous communication between students in the virtual community that can be useful using different types of technologies that will open the door to a social interactive network.

Militaru, Niculescu, and Teaha (2013) suggested that there are not any "hardware acquisition costs, no software licenses or upgrades to pay, no hidden costs, no facilities to lease, no capital costs of any kind. Students and teachers can use only what they want and pay only for what they use" (p. 215). Keeping cost down and interests up will make the virtual community popular as well as a useful resource for teachers and students. By keeping the costs down and not having software licensing upgrades to pay will improve cost efficiency as well as manage budgeting issues.

Militaru, Niculescu, and Teaha (2013) also noted that "studies show that there is a positive relation between student's needs and cloud adoption. According to these results, the following general hypothesis about the relation between academic members and students needs and cloud adoption in universities can be addressed" (p. 215). Cloud service providers can impact the continued use of the environment since the cloud community can develop and grow based on the flow of services. The adoption of the service will impact the decision to which cloud service will be selected.

Figure 6 is an illustration of cloud technology. This illustration shows how different features such as the classroom, student collaboration and the virtual community can impact the adoption of the cloud. Also the interaction between the classroom, student collaboration and the virtual community are impacted by the development of cloud technology. The classroom can be set up by providing access to the classroom along with a setup for managing resources and archiving data. Student collaboration is used to access posts, resources and archives for students.

Development of Cloud Technology

Figure 6. Cloud Technology and Different Parts of Technology

As the development of the cloud is managed by teachers and staff and used by students, it is critical for the virtual community to analyze and evaluate the information with a quality plan. In Chapter 7, there will be a discussion about the importance of using quality assurance to evaluate the virtual community. The development of a quality assurance plan would be useful for evaluating the planning, design, setup, and implementation of the virtual community using cloud technology.

CHAPTER 7.
ENSURING QUALITY ASSURANCE IN THE
E-COLLABORATION OF THE
VIRTUAL COMMUNITY

QA TOOLS AND TECHNIQUES

Quality assurance techniques, tools, and models are needed to ensure success in making decisions for schools, especially as it applies to checking the quality for the cloud and virtual community. Management and teachers will determine how cloud computing and the virtual community will be developed. Managing and evaluating quality techniques and quality tools are a part of the assessment process.

Quality techniques such as statistical quality evaluations deal with "the collection, analysis, and interpretation of data related to the causes of variations in quality characteristics" (Modarress & Ansari, 1989, p. 59). This is an important approach to managing a quality assurance plan for the virtual community. There are various tools that can be used with a quality assurance process. It is important to have an understanding of what the tool are used for and how the tool can be used to provide a quality outcome for the virtual community and cloud service.

Tools such as the scatter diagram, Pareto chart, histogram, frequency histogram, attribute control charts, and variable control charts are some of the basic tools that can be used to evaluate data, services, websites, and applications. As noted in Figures 1 and 2, both the SWOT analysis and the cause-and-effect diagram are quality techniques that would be beneficial for evaluating and monitoring quality. The tools can even be used to improve processes for the cloud and virtual communities.

Not only are quality tools and techniques useful but also statistical measurements can be used to manage the effectiveness of information. Part of the quality process is continuous improvement processes. The continuous improvement process can be used to evaluate the current service and determine whether upgrades or changes to the service are required. Using a continuous improvement process along with a quality plan will help when assessing changes. This can be considered a roadmap for ensuring that all aspects of the virtual community and the cloud service are being evaluated.

QUALITY PLAN

A quality plan is a tool that can be used to manage and strategically align requirements that interpret the data and effectively manage continuous improvement. The quality plan should be used as a guide for ensuring that the environment and cloud services are meeting the expectations of the school. As the quality of the virtual community and cloud service are evaluated against standards and guidelines, teachers input should be included to determine the efficiency and effectiveness of the community.

DEVELOPING A QUALITY PLAN FOR THE VIRTUAL COMMUNITY USING CLOUD TECHNOLOGY

Storr and Hurst (2001) noted that there are some basic steps that can help organizations and businesses set up a useful quality plan. The framework of the quality plan may use six dimensions for quality. One of the dimensions that Storr and Hurst mentioned was the effectiveness of the service. This means that in order for there to be an effective process, product or service, the benefits need to be considered. This can be applied to any situation that is set up where a product, process, or service is evaluated to determine if there are any benefits associated with it.

Additionally, there are five other dimensions that include acceptability, efficiency, accessibility, equity, and relevance. Each of the aforementioned dimensions can be applied and developed as part of a quality plan to evaluate a product, process, or service. Table 1 illustrates the quality dimensions and how they are applicable to the community as well as the cloud.

The virtual community would be considered acceptable if the community demonstrates to individuals that those that use the community are satisfied and that their expectations are met. The efficiency of the community is based on the use of resources and this increases the accessibility, thereby limiting the time or distance that could negatively impact the virtual community. There is also equity and relevance in the community by noting how individuals access the service and how long the service is available.

A quality plan would be useful for evaluating the effectiveness, acceptability, efficiency, accessibility, equity, and relevance of the community and the cloud. Next, a plan and different areas of plan that would be useful in evaluating the community and the cloud are introduced.

Table 1. Quality Dimensions and Applicable Value

Quality dimension	Applicable to community and cloud
Effectiveness	What are the benefits
Acceptability	Satisfaction and expectations
Efficiency	Use of resources
Accessibility	Limits of time or distance
Equity	Treatment of those involved
Relevance	Is the service needed

DETERMINING A PLAN, TOOL, AND TECHNIQUE

Developing a quality plan that is used to manage the strategic planning for the virtual community can be set up using the following elements. The quality plan can be used to guide and manage the quality of the virtual community as well as the cloud environment.

The quality plan may include:

1. Cover page—The cover page should include the project name, date and institution

2. Table of contents

3. Project and personnel

   a. Description of the project and the personnel or positions that will be working with the virtual community and cloud service providers

4. Flowchart of project and personnel

   a. A flowchart showing the chain of events and the chain of command of the personnel or positions of who will be responsible for managing the virtual community and the cloud service provider

5. Training/certifications

   a. Training required—List who will be trained and the form of certification that will be available after the training.

6. Problem to be analyzed

   a. Flowchart showing the current problem and the proposed setup of the virtual community and the positions that will be responsible for managing the cloud services and the virtual community.

7. Process

   a. Flowchart showing how the different positions will be responsible for specific areas in the virtual community and the cloud services.

8. Quality objectives

   a. Management of the community and cloud using quality objectives

9. Quality measurements—Evaluation of different tools available that can be used to assess quality. Different tools can be used to provide information about whether there is a relationship between variables, time, and resources. Figures 1 and 2 are examples of different tools and how they can be used to assess the virtual community. The American Society for Quality provides information on various quality tools that can be useful in evaluating the virtual community and cloud computing—http://asq.org/learn-about-quality/quality-tools.html.

   a. Scatter diagram—pairs of variables that show relationships

   b. Pareto diagram—frequency and cost evaluated in a process

   c. Histogram—frequency or numerical values

   d. Control charts—shows a process over time

   e. Check sheet—can be used to review data over and over at the same time

f. Run chart—evaluate data over time

g. QFD—makes use of different management planning tools

h. Cause and effect—evaluate causes and the effects

i. SWOT analysis—evaluate strengths, weaknesses, opportunities, and threats

10. Maintenance and continuous improvement plan—a plan for developing an approach to evaluating a process, maintenance, and development of a continuous improvement process.

Some examples of quality tools are provided in the following that can be used to evaluate the strategic effectiveness along with the cause and effect of the cloud computing and virtual learning community. Following is an example of a SWOT diagram for the virtual community and cloud computing that was developed to illustrate different areas of strengths, weaknesses, opportunities, and threats.

Figure 1. SWOT Analysis for Virtual Community and Cloud Computing

Following is an example of a cause-and-effect diagram for the virtual community. In this diagram, there is a cause-and-effect relationship shown to illustrate the critical areas to evaluate. For example, the effect may be low participation in the virtual community. Potential causes to evaluate may be: no management, lack of interest, technology out of date, and lack of scheduling. Issues that may impact no management may be the manager or no one in charge. The lack of interest issues may include information that is not useful and accurate. For technology, out-of-date issues may be budget and the technology may be old. Lack of scheduling issues may include scheduling problems and time for all participants. As noted, each of the issues is related to a cause, impacting low participation in a virtual community.

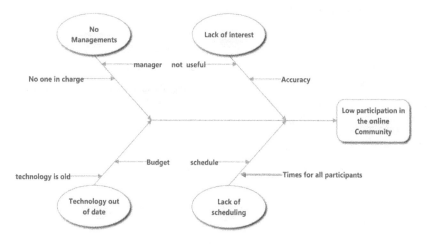

Figure 2. Cause-and-Effect Analysis for Virtual Community and Cloud Computing

Additional areas that may be included in the quality plan are:

11. Quality dimensions/indicators—Each of the indicators presented below, are areas that can be evaluated using quality tools.
    a. Effectiveness
    b. Acceptability
    c. Efficiency
    d. Accessibility
    e. Equity
    f. Relevance
12. Monitoring—Continuing an evaluation of the process in order to make changes

a. Continuous improvement

13. Analysis/evaluation

a. Evaluation of the data and evaluation of the collection of data

14. Assessment/reporting

a. Assessment of the data for reporting

15. Recommendations for improvement as well as continuous improvement

16. Recommendations for the future quality of the community and cloud computing

(The aforementioned is based on a template shown on: http://www.in.gov /idem/nps/3383.htm)

Now that the plan is presented, it is necessary to collect data for analysis.

COLLECT DATA FOR PLAN

The data for the plan can be collected by using the quality plan noted above. A template can be developed using the plan and can be used for measuring, analyzing, and evaluating the progress of the virtual community and the cloud service.

The techniques of quality as noted by Plsek (1995) include plans for improvement along with models for improvement. Also, there are basic tools that are useful for managing quality that include managing teams and projects. Plsek (1995) suggested several different tools for managing quality that include:

- Process tools
- Data collection tools
- Data analysis tools
- Statistical tools
- Collaborative techniques
- Planning techniques

- Management and planning tools
- Customer needs analysis
- Quality function deployment analysis
- Benchmarking

Each of the aforementioned tools, processes, and techniques can be useful for evaluating the site and this will help management determine where and how to make changes. Also, it is important to keep the plan current and up to date in order for it to be an effective tool.

KEEPING PLAN CURRENT

A continual improvement process should be put in place in order to ensure quality improvement. The plan should be reviewed on a regular basis and updated when changes occur. The plan is not useful if it is not kept current and used. It is considered a guide and a strategic approach to keeping up with quality standards. In the next chapter, there will be a discussion about the future of e-collaboration using virtual communities and cloud computing and what can be expected as a future direction.

CHAPTER 8.
FUTURE OF VIRTUAL COMMUNITIES
AND CLOUD COMPUTING

As cloud computing continues to grow, there will be more areas to consider as part of future development, planning, and growth. Arutyunov suggested that "cloud computing is a reflection of global trends on the transition to outsourcing and external services" (Arutyunov, 2012, p. 178). This has created not only a new technology but also opportunities for the development of new Internet options and ways to access information using outsourcing and other external available services.

As noted in Figure 1, technology has opened up a global market and this includes outsourcing as an option for obtaining services. As the global market increases, so does the relationship with "customer and the provider of IT Services" (Arutyunov, 2012, p. 178). This relationship can be used to establish "how and on what models is it more effective to build relationships between the customer and the provider of IT services" (Arutyunov, 2013, p. 178).

As models are developed, working with cloud computing as well as collaborative services will open areas to explore that may include new vendors and suppliers. These suppliers will be able to work with technical aspects of cloud services that include the "Cloud Broker, which is a new layer of suppliers' cloud services" (Arutyunov, 2012, p. 178). This type of broker storage can be used to manage cloud services as well as take care of the management, monitoring, and planning of services.

Since the future of cloud services is an area that will continue to evolve, future advancements in technology as it applies to virtual communities and cloud computing are necessary. Kane et al. (2015) noted that the college or university must be able to determine whether there is a plan for the future that includes a strategic effort and effort for advanced technology. Also, the school may need to understand the culture for determining whether future advancement encourages new techniques that are representative of the work force. As a virtual community, successful planning and training are needed in order to understand how technology works. Technical aspects of cloud services, updates, and changes need to be carefully assessed and monitored.

Individuals in the college and university environment should be trained and given webinars to keep up to date with the purpose and usefulness of the virtual community and how the cloud service can be used for the community (Kane et al., 2015). The future of virtual communities and cloud computing is based on the global presence, culture of the community, and available cloud services. The platform, participants, resources, and the Internet are all critical considerations when evaluating the future growth of the virtual community and cloud computing. Also, it is important to keep the information current and archived as needed.

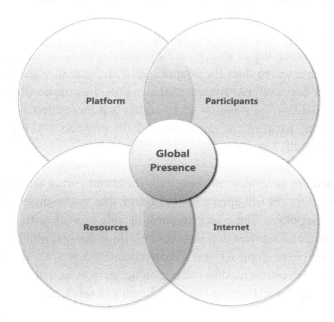

Figure 1. A Global Presence for the Virtual Community and the Cloud Computing

KEEPING INFORMATION CURRENT

Keeping information current can be a challenge for any school, university, or college. Technology has progressed so quickly that schools, colleges, and universities have difficulty keeping up with the advances in technology. Budgets often keep administrators' hands tied when decisions need to be made about the advancement of technology and training that is needed for keeping current with technology.

Myers et al. (2015) discussed how virtual education is trending and that working toward flexible education options is something that has encouraged the advancement of higher education. This advancement has encouraged more and more individuals to go back to school, which has increased and encouraged virtual community collaboration and cohesiveness. As Myers et al. noted, "Factors identified from those studies can be categorized pedagogically as (a) interactive teaching strategies, (b) variety in course delivery methods, and (c) professional socialization via technology" (Myers et al., 2015, p. 651). These factors are all based on the use of technology and are all areas in which future growth can occur and impact the future success of the virtual community.

As virtual education continues, Myers et al. noted that "online and distance learning has become a growing component of higher education, and the need to develop a community of scholars who can collaborate and support each other is critical" (Myers et al., 2015, p. 654). The virtual community will continue to grow along with virtual education if management sees the value of how the virtual community can be used in conjunction with the virtual schools. The collaboration of those working in the virtual community can be used to support future growth and their understanding of how the growth can positively impact the continued growth of virtual education.

Shon et al. (2014) noted that there are areas that will continue to be challenges in the present and the future as they are related to cloud computing. Connectivity and server issues may prohibit the users from using the community so alternatives need to be established so that virtual community users can make alternative choices for connectivity, and security is not a major disadvantage of storing and accessing information on the cloud. Also, hacker attacks can impact the cloud network just as easily as school servers. So evaluating security issues is necessary not only when accessing information on the school servers but also for cloud service. There needs to be a plan in place to deal with both types of security issues in order to keep the community stable.

The stability of the service can impact the community and the providers so services not only for the cloud computing service need to be stable but also for the virtual community. There needs to be adequate storage space and authentication based on data which may have overflow issues (Shon et al., 2014). If there is not enough storage space to house data and there are continual overflow issues, individuals will not want to use the service and will not want to be a part of the virtual community.

A future direction that will impact cloud services and the virtual community is the use of mobile computing. Mobile devices have become an important part of communication and mobile devices are important when considering how to determine access to specific services. Shon et al. noted that "small hand-held devices enable us to connect to the cloud through wireless networks, anywhere. This mobility can cause intermittent connectivity and large variations on latency and data rates" (Shon et al., 2014, p. 409). Since individuals who are using mobile devices are moving around in different areas, connectivity may be an issue. Limited mobility users may find that "wireless connections offer lower data rates compared to fixed networks and can cause a bottleneck for applications that require large data volumes" (Shon et al., 2014, p. 409). If the individual who is using the mobile device relies on this as their technology for connecting then future goals may be to work towards minimizing intermittent connectivity and variations of latency and data rates while increasing storage. Another area that may impact mobile devices includes "power capacity of the mobile device, available bandwidth of the wireless channel, and movement" (Shon et al., 2014, p. 409). Mobile devices in today's society have increased communication but are not without problems when it comes to mobility, storage, and connectivity.

CLOUD SERVICE PROVIDERS

Trends continue to expand and grow and Wang, Rashid, and Chuang (2011) noted that cloud computing is the trend for the future as well as cloud providers that are able to host a variety of services. The cloud service providers as noted previously include three different service types: SaaS, PaaS, and IaaS.

Following are several different services that can be evaluated and assessed for the use of cloud services that are specific for SaaS, PaaS, and IaaS. For SaaS or software as a service, the providers are Salesforce.com or Sale Cloud, and Google has Google Docs, NetSuite has NetSuite CRM+, and Apple has iCloud. With the PaaS platform or the platform as a service Google has Google Aps, Microsoft has Azure, and Salesforce.com uses Force.com. The IaaS or the infrastructure as a service has Amazon with Amazon Services, and Savvis has Colocation hosting and GoGrid has cloud hosting (Wang et al., 2011, p. 239). Table 1 provides a representation of the different cloud architectures and services

Table 1. Cloud Architecture and Services

SaaS—Software as a service	PaaS—Platform as a service	IaaS—Infrastructure as a service
Sale Cloud	Google Aps	Amazon Services
Google Docs	Azure	Colocation
NetSuite CRM+	Force.com	Cloud Hosting
iCloud		

Another area to evaluate is the open-source cloud that is important for looking at public communities. Open-source standards are important for public service. Some examples of open-source cloud computing include AppScale, Cloud Foundry, OpenNebula, and Open Stack. IBM also has IBM Cloud Academy that is used for education and general practitioners for working toward increasing knowledge and awareness in Cloud Computing (Wang et al., 2011, p. 240). The evaluation of the different cloud computing examples is useful for determining the effectiveness and efficiency of the service as well as future direction.

Wang et al. discussed how important it is to understand how cloud computing and the measurement and evaluation of different technologies can be used to determine the effectiveness of the cloud service. As companies look at the growing list of providers, it is essential to also look at the provider's current service, ideas for future growth, limitations in the technology, and business models for future research for not only the businesses but also for the users of cloud services (Wang et al., 2011, p. 241).

When planning for the cloud service and determining a cloud community growth, looking at future growth and how growth will impact the service will become necessary. Evaluating the limitations that users may have as it is related to the state-of-the-art technology will be a concern particularly as cloud services adapt new technology and users are limited to what they can use to access the cloud and virtual communities.

Wang et al. also noted that future trends for cloud services may negatively impact the operation of IT departments in the school while with less service requirement, jobs may be impacted. Jobs may be cut and services may be limited to only the essential support areas for the school. Since security is a continual issue, security risks may impact the housing of data and information. This will need to be managed successfully by the school and the cloud service. In order for this to be an effective project, there needs to be a plan, design, and evaluation of in-house versus cloud computing services. The evaluation should be a statistical evaluation using some of the various statistical tools noted in Chapter 7. This evaluation will be useful in determining the best fit for the school (Wang et al., 2011, p. 241).

The future of technology and the cloud will benefit teachers, students, and staff because the newest technology can help advance the modes of communication and interaction in the school. For example, Adobe Creative Cloud is a service that provides different tools for students and teachers.

As noted from their website—https://creative.adobe.com/plans?promoid =P3KMQZ9Y&mv=other—students and teachers can receive different tools for special pricing unique for teachers and students. For example, for 9.99 a month (prices subject to change), students and teachers can get Photoshop and Light room along with ways to manage and organize photos using the desktop or mobile device. For 19.99 a month (prices subject to change), students and teachers can get a collection of 20 different desktop and mobile applications that includes Photoshop and Illustrator. Also, a portfolio website and 20 GB of cloud storage are provided. This is just an example of services available from a cloud provider.

FUTURE DIRECTIONS

As colleges and universities continue to move toward future trends and changes, keeping current with new technology and new cloud service providers is needed. The evaluation of new services and providers will be beneficial for schools, teachers, and students.

Eunjeong noted that "by 2016, global data center traffic is expected to reach 6.6 zettabytes, a nearly four-fold increase from 1.8 zettabytes in 2011, with cloud traffic representing 4.3 zettabytes (64%), compared to 683 exabytes (39%) in 2011" (Eunjeong, 2013, p. 104). This is quite an increase in traffic and service to accommodate the influx of traffic that will need to be managed.

Eunjeong also noted that "cloud computing is bringing rapid and diverse changes in the use of information. It has five characteristics: (1) on-demand self-service; (2) broadband network access; (3) resource pooling; (4) rapid elasticity or expansion; and (5) measured service" (Eunjeong, 2013, pp. 104, 105). Each of the aforementioned characteristics are areas that need to be tracked and monitored.

For example, individuals want to be ensured that when they want to communicate with a virtual service they have the ability to log on and access the service. Also, Eunjeong (2013) further noted that future changes may include an evaluation of a new selection of services, new and improved devices that can access the cloud, the ability to receive more information, and an increased approach to managing information. These are all areas that will be considered as future technology is developed.

Continually looking at different options for communication and collaboration has opened the door for new technology. That is why it is important to understand how new technology can be used and how it can impact learning. Keeping up to date with new trends and options for communication will continue to grow. Colleges and universities are continually looking for ways to improve skills, knowledge, and learning through different approaches in education. This book has provided some basic elements for evaluating different approaches to collaboration and communication through virtual communities that use cloud technology. This advancement toward online communities and cloud technology has expanded how teachers and students can interact and communicate. This is a preliminary view of how the community can be used by teachers, students, and staff, and hopefully has provided some ideas for future use and growth.

REFERENCES

Alzain, M. A., Soh, B., & Pardede, E. (2012). A new model to ensure security in cloud computing services. *Journal of Service Science Research, 4*(1), 49–70. doi: 10.1007/s12927-012-0002-5

Al-Zoube, M. (2009). E-Learning on the Cloud. *International Arab Journal of e-Technology, 1*(2), 58–64.

Amazon Web Services (2016). *Amazon S3.* Retrieved from http://aws.amazon.com/s3/

American Society for Quality (2016). *Plan-Do-Check-Act (PDCA) Cycle.* Retrieved from http://asq.org/learn-about-quality/project-planning-tools/overview/pdca-cycle.html

Anderson, K., Bastian, J., Harvey, R., Plum, T., & Samuelsson, G. (2011). Teaching to trust: How a virtual archives and preservation curriculum laboratory creates a global education community? *Archival Science, 11*(3–4): 349–372. doi:10.1007/s10502-011-9157-y

Angeles, S. (2014). *Virtualization vs. cloud computing: What's the difference?* Retrieved from http://www.businessnewsdaily.com/5791-virtualization-vs-cloud-computing.html

Armstrong, A., & Thornton, N. (2012). Incorporating Brookfield's discussion techniques synchronously into asynchronous online courses. *Quarterly Review of Distance Education, 13*(1), 1–9, 49–50. Retrieved from http://search.proquest.com/docview/1034104103?accountid=14872

Arutyunov, V. V. (2012). Cloud computing: Its history of development, modern state, and future considerations. *Scientific and Technical Information Processing, 39*(3), 173–178. doi:10.3103/S0147688212030082

Baglieri, D., & Consoli, R. (2009). Collaborative innovation in tourism: Managing virtual communities. *TQM Journal, 21*(4), 353–364. doi: 10.1108/17542730910965065

Beer, M., Slack, F., & Armitt, G. (2005). Collaboration and team-work: Immersion and presence in an online learning environment. *Information Systems Frontiers, 7*(1), 27–37. doi:10.1007/s10796-005-5336-9

Campbell, K., & Ellingson, D. A. (2010). Cooperative learning at a distance: An experiment with wikis. *American Journal of Business Education, 3*(4), 83–89. Retrieved from http://search.proquest.com/docview/195911852?accountid=14872

Campbell, M., & Uys, P. (2007). Identifying success factors of ICT in developing a learning community.*Campus - Wide Information Systems, 24*(1), 17. doi:10.1108/10650740710726464

Cano-Lopez, J. (2005). What is grid computing? *Direct Response* April 2005, p. 21.

Chang, H. (2012). The development of a learning community in an e-learning environment. *International Journal of Pedagogies & Learning, 7*(2), 154-161.

Charalambos, V., & Michalinos, Z. (2004). The design of online learning communities: Critical issues. Educational Media International, 41(2), p. 135, doi: 10.1080/09523980410001678593

Chard, K., Caton, S., Rana, O., & Bubendorfer, K. 2010. *Social cloud: Cloud computing in social networks.* Paper presented at CLOUD 2010: IEEE 3rd International Conference on Cloud Computing 99–106.

Chen, H.-L., Fan, H.-L., & Tsai, C.-C. (2014). The role of community trust and altruism in knowledge sharing: An investigation of a virtual community of teacher professionals. *Educational Technology and Society, 17*(3), 168–179.

Dasgupta, S., Granger, M., & McGarry, N. (2002). User acceptance of E-collaboration technology: An extension of the technology acceptance model. *Group Decision and Negotiation, 11*(2), 87–100.

Diaz, V. (2011). Cloud-based technologies: Faculty development, support, and implementation. *Journal of Asynchronous Learning Networks, 15*(1), 95.

Dillon, T., Wu, C., & Chang, E. (2010, April). *Cloud computing: issues and challenges.* AINA: 24th IEEE International Conference on Advanced Information Networking and Applications, 27–33.

Divya, P., & Prakasam, S. (2015). Effectiveness of cloud based e-learning system (ECBELS). *International Journal of Computer Applications, 119*(6), 29–36.

Drupal (n.d.). *About.* Retrieved from https://www.drupal.org/about

Durand. (2011). *12 community platforms: A list in development.* Retrieved from http://www.freshminds.net/2011/07/12-community-platforms-a-list-in-development/

El-Seoud, M. S. A., El-Sofany, H. F., Taj-Eddin, I. A. T. F., Nosseir, A., & El-Khouly, M. M. (2013). Implementation of Web-based education in Egypt through cloud computing technologies and its effect on higher education. *Higher Education Studies, 3*(3), 62–76. doi: 10.5539/hes.v3n3p62

Eunjeong, C. (2013). How cloud computing is revolutionizing the future. *SERI Quarterly, 6*(3), 104–109, 111.

Get Satisfaction, Inc. (2014). *Online community. The shortest distance between you and your customer.* Retrieved from https://getsatisfaction.com/corp/

Glassmeyer, D.M., Dibbs, R. A., & Jensen, R. T. (2011). Determining utility of formative assessment through virtual community. Perspectives of online graduate students. *Quarterly Review of Distance Education, 12*(1), 23–35, 71–72.

Google (2016) Google apps for work. Retrieved from https://apps.google.com/intx/en_us/pricing.html?

Gupta, S., & Kim, H. (2004). *Virtual community: Concepts, implications, and future research directions.* Retrieved from http://www.virtual-communities.net/mediawiki/images/4/4a/SIGEBZ05-1115.pdf

Heath, B., Herman, R., Lugo, G., Reeves, J., & al, e. (2005). Developing a mobile learning environment to support virtual education communities. T.H.E.Journal, 32(8), 33-34,36-37.

HHS.gov. (2016). *The privacy act.* Retrieved from http://www.hhs.gov/foia/privacy/#

Integrated LMS. (2012). *Integrated LMS LMS + SIS in cloud.* Retrieved from http://www.integratedlms.com/

Isaila, N. (2014). Cloud computing in education. *Knowledge Horizons: Economics, 6*(2), 100–103.

Jabbour, K. K. (2013). Cloud computing concepts for academic collaboration. *Bulgarian Journal of Science and Education Policy, 7*(1), 38–48.

Johnston, R. (2008). Why virtualization? Because it makes business sense. *CPA Technology Advisor, 18*(7), 19–21.

Joshi, R.K., & Ram, D. J. (1999). Anonymous remote computing: A paradigm for parallel programming on interconnected workstations. *IEEE Transactions on Software Engineering, 25*(1), 75–90. doi:10.1109/32.748919

Kane, G.C., Palmer, D., Phillips, A. N., & Kiron, D. (2015). Is your business ready for a digital future? *MIT Sloan Management Review, 56*(4), 37–44.

Keng, C.-J., Hui-Ying, T., & Ya-Ting, C. (2011). Effects of virtual-experience combinations on consumer-related "sense of virtual community." *Internet Research, 21*(4), 408–434. doi: doi.org/10.1108/106622 41111158308

LearningPath.org. (2016). 15 *Free online learning communities.* Retrieved from http://learningpath.org/articles/15_Free_Online_Learning_Communities.html

Lee, Y. (2012). A study on the influence of organizational change on organizational effectiveness of schools: Using investment for cloud computing technologies as a moderator. *African Journal of Business Management, 6*(17), 5710–5719. doi:10.5897/AJBM11.1528

Letitia, T. (2012). Characteristics of the online learning environment organization. Traditional and electronic teaching. In *Leveraging Technology for Learning.* Paper presented at the *Proceedings of the 8th International Scientific Conference eLearning and Software for Education,* Bucharest, April 26–27, 2012. Retrieved from http://proceedings.elseconference.eu/index.php?r=site/index&year=2012&index=papers&vol=1&paper=0ae9942f8852655c55eabb6809286d0c

Martinez, N. (2005, Jan 24). What does the future hold for the grid computing system? *Microscope.* p. 12.

Microsoft (2016). *From SkyDrive to OneDrive.* Retrieved from http://windows.microsoft.com/en-us/onedrive/skydrive-to-onedrive

Militaru, G., Niculescu, C., & Teaha, C. (2013). *Critical success factors for cloud computing adoption in higher education institutions: A theoretical and empirical investigation.* Paper presented at the International Conference on Management and Industrial Engineering, 6 (pp. 213–220), Bucharest: Niculescu Publishing House.

Mitakos, T., Almaliotis, I., Diakakis, I., & Demerouti, A. (2014). An insight on E-learning and cloud computing systems. *InformaticaEconomica,18*(4), 14–25. doi: 10.12948/issn14531305/18.4.2014.02

Modarress, B., & Ansari, A. (1989). Quality control techniques in US firms: A survey. *Production and Inventory Management Journal, 30*(2), 58.

Moodlerooms (2012). *Meet Joule.* Retrieved from http://www.moodle-rooms.com/meet-joule-lms

Mousannif, H., Khalil, I., & Kotsis, G. (2013). Collaborative learning in the clouds. *Information Systems Frontiers, 15*(2), 159–165. doi:10.1007/s10796-012-9364-y

Myers, L. H., Jeffery, A. D., Nimmagadda, H., Werthman, J. A., & Jordan, K. (2015). Building a community of scholars: One cohort's experience in an online and distance education doctor of philosophy program. *Journal of Nursing Education, 54*(11), 650–654. doi:10.3928/01484834-20151016-07

Open Source Matters (2016). *Joomla: The platforms millions of websites are built on.* Retrieved from https://www.joomla.org/

Pappas (2013). *The ultimate list of cloud-based learning management systems.* Retrieved from http://elearningindustry.com/the-ultimate-list-of-cloud-based-learning-management-systems

Pligg LLC (2016). *About Pligg CMS.* Retrieved from http://pligg.com/about/

Plsek, P. E. (1995). Techniques for managing quality. *Hospital and Health Services Administration, 40*(1), 50.

Purch. (2016). *Amazon Cloud Drive Amazon.com, Inc.*, Retrieved from http://cloud-services-review.toptenreviews.com/amazon-cloud-drive-review.html

Raudenbush, D., (2016). GlobalPost *Advantages and disadvantages to learning communities in college.* Retrieved from http://everydaylife.globalpost.com/advantage-disadvantages-learning-communities-college-3540.html

Shon, T., Cho, J., Han, K., & Choi, H. (2014). Toward advanced mobile cloud computing for the internet of things: Current issues and future direction. *Mobile Networks and Applications,19*(3), 404–413. doi:10.1007/s11036-014-0509-8

Software Insider (2016). *Compare cloud computing providers.* Retrieved from http://cloud-computing.softwareinsider.com/

Storr, L., & Hurst, K. (2001). Developing a quality assurance framework for in-service training and development. *Quality Assurance in Education, 9*(3), 132–138. doi: 10.1108/09684880110399086

Thomas, P. Y. (2011). Cloud computing: A potential paradigm for practising the scholarship of teaching and learning. *The Electronic Library, 29*(2), 214–224.

Trent, A. (2016). *Disadvantage of online learning communities.* Retrieved from http://education.seattlepi.com/disadvantage-online-learning-communities-1331.html

Wang, W. Y. C., Rashid, A., & Chuang, H. (2011). Toward the trend of cloud computing. *Journal of Electronic Commerce Research, 12*(4), 238–242.

Wesner, M. S., & Hobgood, A. S. (2012). Virtual collaboration: Exploring the process and technology in a graduate course. *Organization Development Journal, 30*(3), 29.

ZDNet (2016). *Ten leading platforms for creating online communities.* Retrieved from http://www.zdnet.com/article/ten-leading-platforms-for-creating-online-communities/

Zhao, C., & Kuh, G. (2004). *Adding value: Learning communities and student engagement.* Retrieved from http://www.nsse.indiana.edu/pdf/ research_papers/Zhao_Kuh_Learning_Communities.pdf

www.ingramcontent.com/pod-product-compliance
Lightning Source LLC
Chambersburg PA
CBHW071256050326
40690CB00011B/2427